SOLDIER OF TRUTH

SOLDIER OF TRUTH

THE TRIALS OF REV. EDWARD PINKNEY

WITH OTHER STORIES AND COMMENTS BY

PHILIP A. BASSETT

*To my mother, Dorothy, my first
beacon of kindness in this world,
and to my father, James, the first
warning that something was wrong*

Cover photographs courtesy of daymonjhartley.com
Cover Design by Blue Valley Author Services
More at soldieroftruth.com
ISBN 13: 978-0997781502
ISBN 10: 0997781505

Contents

Note to the Reader

Afterword

Note to the Reader

The following is my account of the most powerful and unique man I have ever met. His uniqueness, I believe, stems from a supportive family and a healthy childhood mixed with enough adversity to hone the strongest character. His power appears to come from a solid core of prized personality traits: unbridled courage coupled with kindness that seems effortless, strong ambition, and a deeply embedded sense of fairness. These traits have made him a worthy and long-standing opponent of the moneyed interests in Berrien County, Michigan.

It is not my intention to list the countless injustices that have been visited on Rev. Edward Pinkney by those entities. Rather, I would like to present a group of stories (some of them about me and people I know) to paint a picture of the system that Rev. Pinkney faces, and why people like me support him.

Watching the Pinkney drama unfold has completely changed my view of politics. Witnessing what passes for jurisprudence in his courtroom battles has opened my eyes to the serious problems in our justice system. A lack of response at the appellate level suggests the sickness exists there as well.

My sincerest apologies for Chapter 7. It is the driest chapter in the book, consisting mostly of trial transcripts, but its inclusion was necessary to let readers see what really goes on in a courtroom.

Philip A. Bassett

1

The First Trial

The long wooden benches were filling up rapidly as we made our way into the Berrien County courtroom. Local residents vied for spots alongside of visitors from as far away as Chicago and Detroit. Most were supporters of Rev. Edward Pinkney, a man I had met a month earlier and liked immediately. The remainder were reporters who were allowed to sit in the front row and a few other interested parties. Despite the hard seats, unfriendly lighting and generally soul-deadening atmosphere, a buzz of anticipation filled the room.

The reporters' pew was crowded; six or seven of us had to cram into it, along with the camera and tripod I had borrowed from the local cable access station. We were situated behind the jury box so the camera wouldn't catch the jurors' faces. I glanced at the bookish, gray-haired reporter next to me and tried a bit of conversation.

"Do you think he did it?" I asked, innocently.

The fierceness of her gaze surprised me. She practically spat out, "Do you know that he's been to prison?" with such venom I thought she might burst a blood vessel in her face.

It was obvious from her response that she already despised this man as much as I was beginning to like him.

What was going on here? I went to look for the reverend. I found him in the lobby, chatting and joking with reporters. He didn't seem worried or depressed. In fact, he seemed like the happiest person in the place, not like a man who was about to go to trial. He smiled at everyone, even the ones who were trying to send him to prison.

I asked if he had ever been to prison before and he immediately said, "Yes," but that he had been set up. I was glad he was candid with me but questioned the part about his being framed. He said he was once an insurance agent and was accused of embezzling money from a client. When he mentioned further details and the amount of money involved, I tended to believe he was, in fact, set up. I was once a licensed agent myself and know that every agency is required to carry Errors and Omissions insurance, just to cover that sort of accusation. The usual amount of coverage is for $1,000,000 or more, which would have easily covered the paltry amount he was accused of taking.

Something wasn't adding up here. In time, two key ingredients would make the whole picture clearer: Pinkney's consistent activism and the evidence of corruption in the Berrien County courthouse, both of which are extensive. But we're getting ahead of our story.

I slipped back into the packed courtroom and found my seat. As I recall, the judge was a little late, so we all sat waiting. Guard cops with arrogant, pushy expressions lined the walls, ready to pounce on whomever broke the rules, of which there were many: no chewing gum, don't talk too loudly, no reading novels, only court materials. It looked like it was going to be a long day.

As it turned out, Judge Alfred Butzbaugh was not overly late and soon got the wheels of justice rolling. The judge moved with the easy assurance of someone who had done this a thousand times. He looked and acted like a kindly old pope as he joked and schmoozed with the jurors. He appeared to be sincere and genuinely concerned, and seemed to almost bend over backwards to accommodate their schedules. His voice was low and croaky, which further softened his appearance. It also had the effect of making those listeners in the first few rows strain to make out consonants, while those further away gave up the effort all together.

At first glance, the judge appeared pretty harmless, but I was among those who would feel the sting of his iron hand before it was all over.

Lunch time was approaching by the time the jury was briefed and opening arguments presented. Afternoon brought the first nuggets of courtroom drama: reams and reams of phone records, laboriously dictated by the junior prosecutor, Gerald Vigansky. In fact, he spent the better part of two days riffling through the reverend's cell phone records, spending extra time whenever the city clerk's number came up.

The clerk, Jean Nesbitt, was the picture of grace on the witness stand. The expression on her face was kind, yet firm and her manner was thoughtful, calm and professional. She had been fired the year before because it was alleged she had somehow helped the recall of Glen Yarbrough come about. However, both of her assistants would testify at this trial that they tabulated all the absentee ballots, thus Mrs. Nesbitt would not have had a reason to handle them.

Apparently, she and the reverend had spoken on the phone several times in the week or so surrounding the election. The young prosecutor picked each phone record clean, recounting the call's duration, and then asking about the conversation. "Yes," Jean said, "We were talking about the election." What else would they be talking about? And how would talking on the phone affect the results of a recall election?

Why anyone would want to impugn this impeccably mannered woman was beyond me, and how she could have helped the reverend's cause, beyond encouragement, remained unclear. As the trial wore on, that disturbing lack of clarity would emerge again and again in the prosecutor's case, eventually becoming the very cornerstone of it.

When Rev. Pinkney took the stand, there were murmurs of approval from the audience, an expectation, perhaps, that his words might inject some sanity into this proceeding. After all, Pinkney was fighting for them, too, and the rest of the three hundred fifty people who had voted to recall Glen Yarbrough. (Three hundred voted against recall.) They knew a judge in this courthouse had somehow wielded astronomical powers and struck down the commissioner's recall on the basis of only five or six so-called "tainted" votes. Perhaps they figured if anyone could stand up to this nonsensical court system, it would be this religious man who wasn't afraid of a political fight.

However, many would learn at this trial that courtrooms are like a world unto themselves; the average person is not privy to their inner workings. We walk into what appears to be a level playing field which quickly converts to a stacked house. Those of us who haven't experienced a trial like this aren't aware of the tremendous advantage the government has in terms of time, resources and manpower, as well as the ability to intimidate potential witnesses. I would argue the government has a moral advantage as well; many feel if a person is on trial, they must have done something wrong. Most of us are overwhelmed by the sheer power of government, and at the same time, we want to like and believe in our leaders. (We also want to be liked by them.) A prosecutor with a few tricks up his sleeve, along with a compliant judge, might be enough to sway a jury.

Prosecutor Vigansky, it seems, had several strategies at his disposal, including the Bait and Switch and Hire a Liar. But his main tactic for now continued to be to Overwhelm with Irrelevant Data. He hammered the reverend with questions about his cell phone records, citing length of calls, then asking details of conversations. Pinkney answered the best he could.

Incidentally, if anyone out there knows how to reverse an election by calling the city clerk, please let the Berrien County justice department know, so that in the future, a judge doesn't have to do it his way. But as it stood, this looked like a day-long invasion of the reverend's privacy.

The young prosecutor continued to champion irrelevance as he made pains to point out particular stamps and stickers that kept showing up on the ballot envelopes. The implication, again, was unclear. Was he saying that since Pinkney provided the stamps, he must have touched the envelopes? Why not take fingerprints and settle the issue conclusively? Apparently real, tangible evidence had no place in the government's case. Pinkney, for his part, freely admitted to handing out stamps to those who needed them, to help in the election effort. As it turns out, the stickers were simply the address where the absentee ballots were to be mailed. These stickers are helpful, because a lot of times, where you obtain the absentee ballot is not the same place it is mailed to.

After several hours examining this non-angle, Vigansky switched to—you guessed it—the Bait and Switch. This mind-numbing strategy consisted of spending hours (and hours) of courtroom time comparing handwriting on the applications for the absentee ballots. Apparently, this was the prosecutor's clever way of boring the crap out of everyone present, and never revealing a scrap of information. Here's why: anyone can fill in your application for an absentee ballot; all you have to do is sign it, and you're entirely within the law. The charges against the reverend involved the ballot itself, but the prosecutor continually paraded applications before witnesses and asked them to compare handwriting, as if it mattered. The switch from ballots to applications made the entire line of questioning pure hogwash, but it was misleading enough to muddle the jurors' minds.

The fragile glue that held the prosecutor's case together was the extended testimony of one witness, a Brenda Fox. Unfortunately, many of the statements Brenda made at this trial almost entirely contradicted testimony she had sworn to in an affidavit a year earlier. On the stand she said simply, "I lied before and now I thought I'd better tell the truth, so now I'm telling the truth."

The story the prosecution presented was that Ms. Fox was a "ringleader" of sorts, rounding up homeless people for Rev. Pinkney and paying them five dollars to vote. Pinkney countered that he did pay certain people five dollars, but it was to hand out flyers announcing the election.

There's no question that one of Brenda's recountings under penalty of perjury was a lie, but which one? And if she's telling the truth now, why wasn't she ever charged with anything?

This was interesting: at the beginning of the trial, there were fifteen jurors, a number later reduced to the required twelve. Apparently, it was assumed the trial would be long and one or two of them might not be able to make the full commitment. When it came time to deliberate, the court recorder brought out an old wooden box and proceeded to drop three numbered tiles out of it, one at a time. The jurors whose numbers were called were sent home. Rev. Pinkney commented later that one of the ousted jurors seemed to be the most empathetic with him, listening closely and sometimes smiling at what he said. He was sorry to see her go. I remember thinking how easily that box could have been rigged. Everything else seemed fishy about this trial, why not that?

Thusly trimmed, the panel of twelve set to the difficult task of judging their peer. It was now entering the third week of the trial, and many in the audience were showing fatigue from the long proceedings. I'm sure members of the jury felt that way, too, but they pondered the evidence (or lack of it) for the better part of two days, finally sending a note to Judge Butzbaugh that they couldn't decide on a verdict. The judge called them out before him and asked if they couldn't try a little harder to reach a decision. They promised to try, but after another day or so of deliberating, the final result was a hung jury with ten jurors wishing to convict. There were two black jurors on the final panel. Was that a coincidence? I don't know. But the Berrien County courthouse would make sure that wasn't an issue the next time they took a swat at the reverend.

As it was, Prosecutor Vigansky convinced ten members of the jury that Rev. Pinkney had committed crimes worthy of twenty years in prison. Granted, being a juror is a heavy responsibility; it's easy to second guess if you're not actually faced with the decision, but the following should give thinking people reason to pause:

1. It seems strange that you can earn five years in prison for having someone else's absentee ballot in your possession; you don't even have to have tampered with it. If you didn't tamper with it, what's the harm? And if you did tamper with it, we already have laws to deal with that!
2. The state's star witness at this trial gave a sworn statement a year earlier that contradicted her entire testimony.
3. The state claimed Pinkney handled certain ballots, yet they never provided a single fingerprint. If he licked envelopes, there was no DNA. If he filled in the blanks on applications (not the ballot itself, and therefore, not a crime), where's the handwriting expert? There wasn't one.

When push came to shove, the government made a lot of accusations with no attempt to prove anything. Hard, tangible evidence was conspicuously absent. Their witnesses were questionable, and they deliberately misled the jury by confusing applications with actual ballots. If that deception was necessary, what else were they hiding? Was the entire three-week trial just a way to neutralize a troublesome dissident? If so, what kind of man draws so much enmity from the government? To shed light on these questions, it might help to look a little closer at the life of Rev. Edward Pinkney.

2

Born to Lead

People speak of made leaders; no doubt there are some, whether they've been carefully coached, lovingly nurtured or simply shaped by events that are thrust upon them. Truly inspired leaders, however, appear to be born that way. It's as if the blueprint for a life of leadership already exists within them, and they arrive fully hardwired for the task. Edward Pinkney seems to have been destined to be a leader from the very beginning. It's evident he's made from sterling stuff—a more loving fighter would be hard for me to imagine. His boundless confidence points to a secure and happy childhood, and the racial turbulence of the 1960's would present more than enough opportunities for a stellar young black man to shine. Again and again, he would be called to bring his special brand of leadership to the table, sometimes with amazing results.

Although I spoke to Rev. Pinkney numerous times in the course of his trials for voter fraud and the years following, it took a long time to piece together the life details of this unique individual. There are a couple of reasons for this. Certain events from his past present automatic red flags for some; he's been in a few fights and he's been to prison. More importantly, although he's obviously comfortable with the man he has grown into, he rarely talks about himself. His conversation is ever focused on injustices people are facing, and what action we might take. When he's not speaking about it, he's taking political action, such as watching court or leading marches.

Learning about his early life would have to wait, as he wound up going to trial a second time, was convicted and sentenced to home confinement, and then later sent to prison over a newspaper article. While incarcerated, he would be nominated to run for Congress on the Green Party ticket. At this time also, the ACLU would step in and work to successfully appeal his sentence, allowing him to leave prison five months later.

Not long afterward, he would be elected president of his local chapter of the NAACP, only to become disillusioned with their lack of action, ultimately resulting in his suing the organization over election irregularities.

Around this time, we were able to hold a series of interviews at the local library, and he told me about his early life.

Born in 1948, he grew up the middle child of nine on Chicago's north side, during an era when mothers could afford to stay home with their children. He says he loved his whole family, but was especially close with his two brothers, Fred and Jim, who were next to him in age. They did everything together "that needed to be done," whether it was baseball, studying, or fighting.

In 1959, his father, who was also named Edward, and his mother, Desiree, moved the family of eleven to the west side of Chicago. With the move came a change in demographics, and they found themselves in the minority at school. At first, every day after school, a large group of white kids (the whole school, he says) would follow him and his brothers home. It sounds frightening to me, but he says that he and his brothers weren't afraid. "They knew not to mess with us," he recalls. Things escalated one day when a neighbor tried to goad his son into fighting one of the Pinkney boys. The son refused, saying he was their friend!

When the reverend recalls the event, it's from the angle of someone who's used to winning people's respect. "That was really how we broke that up," he explains, commenting on the tension at the time. "They realized that we were no threat to them, but we were willing to fight." That proved to be a winning recipe for peaceful, even convivial, relations with their new neighbors.

Young Edward was making strides at school as well. He remembers taking something called the Constitution Test when it came time to enter the ninth grade. School legend had it that no one had ever gotten a perfect score on the test; the highest up until that time was 95%. Edward and his brothers competed in all areas and this test was no exception. They vowed to be the first to score 100%.

Being older, Fred's turn at the test came first. Studying exhaustively, he was able to match the previous high score of 95%, and yet he came away angry and frustrated. Seeing this made Edward more determined than ever to earn a perfect score. When the time came, he and a friend studied long hours together and took the test with the confidence that comes with ample preparation. When the results came in, Edward's friend, like Fred before him, matched the previous high score. Edward, however, had done the impossible, scoring a perfect 100%.

Rather than being pleased, though, his teacher became suspicious. It seems the test had a gimmick that, until that point, no student had caught on to: five of the questions had no correct answer. The fact that young Edward, an African American, or as they might say back then, colored boy, had figured it out was unthinkable. His teacher accused him of breaking into school at night and sneaking a look at the answers.

His father was called in, and it looked like the young man might be in trouble. The teacher was in for a surprise, though. Mr. Pinkney quietly explained that he called home from work every night at 8:00 and spoke to all the children. It would have been almost impossible for his son to do as they suggested. The young scholar was vindicated, and he says he had a bit of a star status at school after that.

Early on, Edward Pinkney was getting used to occupying that peculiar place we assign to heroes, a space we like to look at but rarely seem to visit. If there was a fight in his neighborhood, he says he was usually called to either mediate or finish it. His leadership ability on the basketball court in high school was noticed by then Mayor Richard Daly, which later resulted in a job. As an eighteen-year-old freshman in college, his stature had elevated such that the Dean of Students asked him to mediate in a major crisis on campus.

He was at West Texas State "living comfortably" on a basketball scholarship, "Minding my own business," he says. Just a few weeks after his first semester started, he was pulled out of class by two older students who directed him to the dean's office. It turned out the dean was in need of a big favor.

It seems that forty or so black students, mostly athletes, had barricaded themselves in the Science building and had been holding it for several hours. The dean wanted the freshman athlete to talk to them and Edward agreed to try.

As he remembers it:

> When I got up there, the first thing I did was ask them what they wanted. (I said) "You're wanting these drastic changes, but you're about to get kicked out of school! That's the number one thing. And then you're going to jail!" So they kind of said, well, I guess they didn't think ahead. I told them, "The number one thing is, you don't want to get kicked out of school, and number two, you don't want to go to jail! Those are the top two. Then you put your demands down after that."

Pinkney left them to mull over his advice. In the meantime, he came out of the building bluffing, shaking his head and muttering how serious the students were about their cause. Perhaps he sensed some fear from the dean and was already playing on it. In truth, many of the students were probably already tiring of the affair and would have liked to see a quick solution. Still, backing down now would mean certain arrest and expulsion. It was clear the students needed an advocate if they were to avoid that, and Edward Pinkney filled the role perfectly.

He acted as a go-between through the standoff's long hours, helping the students hone their strategy and stressing to them the importance of timing. He listened to their concerns, and found a major point was that students of color were often afraid to go to the nearest town of any size. The closest one was fifteen or twenty miles from campus. If one wasn't careful in those days, a black person could end up missing, badly beaten, or dead. The students wanted some assurance of safety when going back and forth to town.

The university's position was they could do nothing to protect the students. Pinkney knew the protesters would have to tread carefully, simply to return to square one. Instinctively, he sought to level the playing field, to make the discussion more meaningful. He exaggerated the strength of the students' resolve and how far they would go. At just the right time, he gave the dean a little nudge:

> I said to him, "If you want them to come out, you are going to have to tell them you're not going to kick them out of school. Or else y'all are going to have to charge the building!" One or the other. So he said, well, he couldn't really make that decision himself. He said he had to go to the board. And I said, "Well, you need to make the decision." I was eighteen. I said, "You need to make that decision, because if you go to the board, you can report to them that you resolved it." That was me talking. I used the word 'resolved' you see, because I knew if they brought in other folks, it wasn't going to happen.

That turn of phrase seemed to help the dean make up his mind. He called the students down to negotiate, agreeing not to expel or prosecute anyone. He also agreed to look into some sort of protection for trips to town. It was a satisfactory way to end a tense, drawn out day, and Pinkney's accomplishment was noted and appreciated by both sides.

Ironically, he would eventually lose his own chance at a degree. He ended up hanging out more with that particular group of students, quickly assuming a role as a leader or spokesman. Although he did passably well in school and sports, racial tensions in the 1960's were such that a racial slur could quickly turn into a full-out fight. In his third year, a large, racially motivated fight broke out at a fraternity on campus and Edward was drawn into it. By then, his standing with the dean had tarnished somewhat, and when it came time to blame someone for the fight, Pinkney was scapegoated. He decided to bow out, losing his chance of graduating from West Texas State.

Accepting his losses, Edward flew home to Chicago and forged on. He tried the insurance business and found that he liked it, soon becoming an excellent salesman.

Meanwhile, one of Mayor Daly's aides contacted him about a job with the city. His duties could be as simple as doing minor research or even just holding a shovel for a promotional photo of City Hall. His office was on the top floor, not far from the mayor's, and he was soon exposed to the inner workings of big-city politics, lessons he applied in his own political battles later on. A somewhat more practical political lesson, however, arrived in the form of Mayor Daly's death. When the new mayor stepped in, Pinkney found his desk had been moved from the top floor down to the basement. The writing was on the wall and he knew it was time to go.

His search for greener pastures led him to go to California in 1984, where he stayed until 1989. He doesn't talk much about these years, except to say that he did get into a fight there. He mentions this fact, not because he's proud (or ashamed) of it, but because to omit it would be a lie. Part of the problem, he says, is that coming from Chicago, people expected him to be tough. Also, as an insurance agent, he became unavoidably involved to varying degrees in his client's lives. When he heard about problems they had, his first impulse was always to help.

In California, one of his clients was a young lady who was having some trouble. On her walk home from work, two men would regularly harass her. Edward offered to walk her home on a daily basis, an offer that was accepted.

The men teased her about her "new boyfriend," but as long as he was with her, that was all. After a week or so of this, he was unable to attend her one day. She later told him that the men had harassed her again.

Continuing to walk her home daily, one day he arrived a few minutes late, just in time to see the men hassling her. He confronted them and a fight broke out. Looking back, he says it was "pretty bloody" and doesn't like to give a lot of details. But those two men never bothered his client again.

Although I've known the reverend since 2005, it was several years before I heard that story. He tells it cautiously, knowing the stigma attached to violent behavior, even when justified. Already routinely battered by the press in his hometown of Benton Harbor, Michigan, he's hesitant to give them more negative fodder.

There are other details of his life missing as well. For instance, I've never heard him mention the mother of his children. Perhaps this is out of respect for his current wife, partner and soul mate, Dorothy. Although he keeps in touch with his kids (they're all adults now), they rarely come up in our conversations. They live out of state, and I think he can relax more because of that. He has some powerful enemies that, from what I've seen, would stop at almost nothing to shut him up. In this book, although we tell a little history, we'll focus mainly on his political stands and their consequences. Let's pick up the story when he arrives in my hometown, Kalamazoo.

3

The Attorney Turn Around

I didn't know Edward Pinkney when we briefly shared the same town in the early 1990's. His victories were already making the news, but I had no idea who the force was behind them.

Pinkney had arrived in Kalamazoo a year or two before I did, finding an insurance sales position and quickly becoming a top performer. Soon many of his clients realized he believed in justice and would fight for it. Some began coming to him for help and advice.

More than one had sobering tales. One lady's son, Beryl Wilson, was arrested on his way to work. He had picked up two friends and was giving them a ride to the store to collect the deposit on the cans and bottles they were carrying. The police stopped them and arrested all three.

While Beryl was in jail, he testified he was made to take off all his clothes, then hosed down and left naked in a cell for several hours. Persistent reports had it that he wasn't the first black man to receive that kind of treatment in the Kalamazoo city jail. In fact, Beryl's mother was in contact with other mothers whose sons reported the same kind of treatment.

Pinkney suggested they get as many people as they could to call the police station and make a complaint. He then made an appointment with the chief of police, Gary Hetrick, and confronted him with the issue. At first, Chief Hetrick flatly denied that anything like that was going on. Pinkney expected that response but still held to his convictions. He was inclined to believe the young men because, for one thing, there were several of them telling the same story. He let the chief know he would be watching the department and left. He says he had a second meeting with the chief but it went nowhere, leaving both men angry.

At this point, Pinkney took no further action, but then Chief Hetrick called him and arranged a meeting. The chief asked him to bring along a few of the young men with stories to tell. Pinkney managed to find three men who were willing to go and face Hetrick. This meeting, however, had a different flavor; the law man humbled himself and actually apologized. The three men each gave their story, and by this time, Chief Hetrick was starting to turn around. He asked them to identify the officers involved, but as that would put more pressure on the young men, Pinkney suggested that it was the chief's responsibility to find out who was on duty at the time. Hetrick agreed to this and the meeting ended amicably.

There was a fourth meeting, and at that time, the chief reassured him this would not happen again, thereby seeming to admit some culpability. Pinkney took that back to Beryl, Mrs. Wilson and the other families, urging them to sue the city. Beryl was one of three who settled with the city, and his compensation was hardly worth the effort. His settlement came to $24,000, but he ended up losing his job as a janitor in the process, and eventually, leaving town.

Pinkney, meanwhile, had relocated to Benton Harbor, Michigan. While working with those families in Kalamazoo, he had come in contact with the Black Autonomy Network of Community Organizers, or BANCO, for short. He would end up practically making the organization his own, infusing it with his boundless energy and tireless networking. He would also meet the woman who would become his soulmate and wife, the lovely Dorothy Williams. Together, along with many others, they would battle the forces trying to repress Benton Harbor residents and stealing the ground from right under their feet.

Pinkney had encountered racism in some form all his life, but even he wasn't ready for what awaited him in Benton Harbor. The racial divide between Benton Harbor and St. Joseph, its sister city across the river, is extreme to the point of being surreal. Statistics like racial makeup, education, income and crime read like a Jekyll and Hyde account. For instance, jobs are practically non-existent in Benton Harbor, as are white people, but both proliferate in sunny St. Joseph across the river. There's no crime in St. Joe but the courthouse is there. It's the colossal cement fortress you see when first crossing the bridge from Benton Harbor. It stands as a stark monument to non-compassion and unrestrained prejudice. Young, mostly black captives are taken there daily to be lied to, intimidated and betrayed by court-appointed attorneys, and then funneled into prison and other programs for profit.

Pinkney had heard the stories of crooked judges and drug-planting cops, but the "straw that broke the camel's back," he says, was an incident that occurred in 1997. There was another intimidator in those days, before the

23

bridge was widened and divided, an ever-present police cruiser right at the St. Joseph end. Levarst Hullet, Jr. was riding his bicycle that day, right past the police car, when the officer decided to stick his arm out and arrest the black man's progress. The hit tumbled Lavarst to the ground and he woke up in the hospital.

When word about the incident got out, St. Joseph officials knew they would have to do some damage control. Police from both sides of the river came together and met with several ministers from Benton Harbor. They wanted the religious leaders to control their flocks and maintain calm. The main message was, "This is St. Joe's business—let us handle it."

Although not yet a minister, Pinkney managed to attend that meeting. He saw the leaders fold to the officer's demands, and pretended to go along. In private, though, he urged the victim to get a lawyer. Lavarst did, and the attorney was able to get a copy of the police tape showing the assault. Video evidence of the officer's action was enough to enflame the hearts of many Benton Harbor residents. Mr. Hullet ended up winning an out-of-court settlement of $35,000 but was picked up six months later by police and ended up serving time in prison.

Now, here's where the story gets weird, and if you choose not to believe it, I'll understand. This was told to me by Rev. Pinkney and corroborated only by his wife. Even so, I give it more weight than ten thousand lawyers and judges testifying at a congressional subcommittee. I've known Rev. Pinkney since 2005, and I've never met a braver man who has so much room in his heart for other people. In my mind, he has no reason to lie.

Additionally, I've been changed by my experience with the courts in Pinkney's case. It appears that when the government wants a particularly troublesome (for whatever reason) individual out of the way, they have several avenues to do so. They can merely call you to court, which stops most of us in our tracks, and make you spend more money than you have. While you're there, they can use the fullest force of the law to intimidate you into taking whatever they offer you. They can construct a jury of your "peers," none of which are the same race as you. If you, the wayward citizen, still insist on having a trial, they can pay witnesses to lie against you. If those witnesses have a change of heart and decide to tell the truth, there are ways of convincing them otherwise, like arresting a relative.

Of course, to do all these things, one has to get you in court in the first place, and if charges aren't readily available, one has to make them up. Every evil propagandist knows that the best way to take someone down is to go after one of their strengths and somehow turn it into a weakness. In Pinkney's case, he was a crackerjack insurance agent, a top performer who really cared about his clients. So he was naturally surprised when police showed up at his house in January of 1999 and told him he was under arrest for embezzlement. They claimed he had mishandled a client's money and failed to turn in the premium in a timely way.

Pinkney says it was a complete fabrication and I believe him for two reasons: one, as I said, I've been an insurance agent and know that every agency has to carry something called Errors and Omissions insurance to cover such mishaps, even those running into thousands of dollars. The other reason is that the charge involved a sum of less than $150. Edward probably could have corrected that with the cash in his wallet.

Despite the flimsiness of the charge, the Berrien County authorities pursued the case confidently and brought Edward Pinkney to trial. Pinkney, choosing to fight, hired an expensive attorney named Peter Johnson, who would later show just how expensive he was.

Pinkney, for his part, was also confident because, he says, he hadn't done anything wrong! His confidence increased as the trial progressed because he felt his answers rang truer than the other witnesses'. Apparently, the courts thought so, too, as they abruptly switched to another tactic, one I'll call the Attorney Turnaround. This involves turning around so quickly one forgets what the truth is, and then it's okay to say anything. It was a bold move, and Pinkney never saw it coming.

"You just perjured yourself," his attorney turned and said to him at one point in the trial. "The penalty for that is up to fifteen years."

Pinkney was aghast, thinking it wasn't possible for him to have done that. However, in the pressures of a trial, he thought, anybody could make a mistake.

"What did I say?" he asked his attorney. "Read back the transcript."

As easy as this would have been, Mr. Johnson didn't read it back; he simply insisted that Pinkney had perjured and he was going to prison for a long time.

Pinkney, bewildered, was herded into a back room and offered a deal. Things had seemingly been going well in the courtroom and he hated to give up the fight. He was confused and intimidated, and not really sure if he had perjured or not. But fifteen years in prison is a very long time...

He agreed to plead guilty with a maximum penalty of 18 months. After he pled guilty, the character and arrogance of the court quickly became evident. Judge Hammond completed the Attorney Turnaround and brought things back to rights.

"You really didn't perjure yourself," he said.

With that, they hauled Edward Pinkney off to live where more than two million Americans now reside: in a cage.

4

Hearing the Call

Of the many reasons I feel a kinship with Edward Pinkney, one of the strongest is that we've both had at least one experience we'd call spiritual. Writing about a spiritual experience can be risky business; I know how people's eyes glaze over when I speak of my own.

In my case, there's not much to tell. It was a summer evening around twenty years ago, and I was home alone. My wife and two daughters were at her parents' up north. I was sitting on my bed in the semi-darkness, a little lonely, trying to meditate and not doing very well at it. All of a sudden, I was visited by such a profound sense of peace, I knew there had to be a presence there. It was around me and inside me and I remember thinking, "I'll never be afraid of the dark again." There was no room for fear within that all pervading peace. I haven't felt anything like it before or since. Even as I've tried to recall it, it's hard to capture the feeling or relive the experience. And I can't, for the life of me, tell you how long it lasted. It could have been thirty seconds or ten minutes. That part seems to escape me. But I live with the confidence that something exists which can wipe away every speck of fear inside me. When people ask me if I believe in God, I say no, I *know* that God exists, or at least something so personal, powerful and wonderful there is nothing to be afraid of ever, and there are certainly no unhappy endings, ultimately, for anyone.

Armed as I am with this awareness, I still find prison hard to stomach. I've spent a few hours in jail on two different occasions and both stays affected me deeply. The first time I was nineteen, drunk, scared, guilty and sorry. I never stole beer again. The second time I was forty, claustrophobic, indignant, and in my mind, not guilty. I only spent a few hours in that marbled holding tank, but I could feel my heart being slowly pulverized by the sheer denial of my humanity there. Luckily, my wife was able to borrow the $100 cash from our neighbor, though it was after midnight. I could hardly wait to feel the outside around me again, so I cringe to imagine what Edward Pinkney felt like when he entered Jackson prison, tried and convicted of a questionable crime.

He says he was angry at first, thinking of ways he could get back at those who had put him there. Normally very active, it frustrated him to gear down to a prison life of very little stimulation, and the huge question kept burning in his head, "Why am I here?"

Underneath the frustration and anger, though, he was aware of a growing excitement. At first he couldn't explain it, but gradually, an understanding began to form. A freak incident had brought him to prison, a supposed crime that no agent he knew had ever been charged with. (His later charge of voter fraud would share the same flavor.) He was confined, but not suffering; in fact, he was as comfortable as could be under the circumstances. Though he was a low security risk, he was placed in level

2 quarters, which allowed him to have his own cell. It was the perfect place for an on-the-go man to slow down and look within, and he began to suspect it had been arranged on purpose.

Things kept happening to confirm his hunch. He was able to visit the law library every day, a status no other inmate enjoyed. (His studies were later instrumental in getting his early release.) A minister saw something special in him and singled him out for private talks. A vision began to take shape, one where he saw himself as part of something bigger, maybe something miraculous, and that made him slow down and pay more attention. As a life-long reader of the Bible, he now had more time to study it. He spent the hours in his cell praying and contemplating. Then one night, he says, something unusual happened. I'll let him tell it in his own words—the following is an excerpt from a June 2013 interview:

Bassett: You heard a voice?

Pinkney: Yeah. It was like a sit-down talk. You sit down on the bed; you can't go nowhere, you're locked up in the cell, and you're able to communicate. You listen to this voice, and the first thing you say is, well, I know it's God—I'm not crazy.

B: You heard an actual voice?

P: Yeah, absolutely. So I'm sitting there hearing a voice and it's telling me what I'm going to do.

B: Can you tell me what it said?

P: It said, "You're going to do some work and most people are not going to like you. But you're going to be doing my work. I want you to just do what you have to do for the people." Maybe not in those exact words.

B: Okay.

P: That's what I got out of it. And then it said—this is the part that got me—it said, "You're going to be leaving here pretty soon." That got my attention.

That last comment had startled him because, as far as he knew, his eighteen-month sentence was written in stone. The part about people disliking him didn't make sense either, as all his life he had been surrounded by people and generally felt that others enjoyed his company. Time, however, would prove the predictions accurate. Edward Pinkney would begin his work of exposing the broken court system in Berrien County; he would lead marches and protests and a campaign to recall a local commissioner. Along the way, corporate and government officials would grow to hate him and seek to neutralize him by any means possible. One of their tactics would be a vicious smear campaign that I believe persists to this day, prompting, say, people in my hometown of Kalamazoo to hate a man who lives 50 miles away, though they have no idea of his views or activities.

As it turned out, he wouldn't have to wait long to start his new life. Through his studies in the law library, he learned of a program that provided for early release in special cases. Because of his mislabeled status, prison officials didn't think he qualified but a call to Lansing soon cleared that up. And although some inmates had waited months, or even years, for a chance at this program, Edward was fast-tracked through in a matter of weeks and was soon on his way home.

Not, however, before he had a chance to preach his first sermon, in Hiawatha Prison in the upper peninsula of Michigan. Then, less than three months after he had entered prison, he was released to start his new life as the Reverend Edward Pinkney.

5

Pushing to the Limit

Back home, he and Dorothy joyfully reunited. She'd been his most loyal supporter, making that critical call to Lansing to gain his release. Now she would be his constant companion as he organized protests and other actions. She would be needed, too, to travel out of town with him when the word spread and he began to make speeches. Always she would answer the call with her infinite patience and quiet strength. Such faithfulness implies a deeply held mission, and Mrs. Pinkney says that she, too, received a brief divine call while her husband was in prison.

"I was going into prayer," she says, and I love the way she puts that. It suggests the creating of a space where listening and understanding can take place. She says she spent the better part of it, though, fretting about some minor problem, and when she was done praying, she still wasn't satisfied. She resolved to take the matter up with Edward when she got the chance. It was then she heard a voice.

"Leave him alone," the voice said. Dorothy was confused, not sure how to feel about what had just happened. She stood there, wavering.

"LEAVE HIM ALONE!" it said, more insistently, and that was all Dorothy Pinkney needed. From then on, she decided to trust whatever action her husband might take, resolving not to drain his energy with doubts and worries, but rather, lend him strength and help him see it through. She continues that practice to this day, and has no peer in this regard.

While her husband was in prison, Dorothy had reestablished contact with BANCO, the organization Edward had become acquainted with when he took the police chief to task in Kalamazoo. With his boundless energy and enthusiasm, the new reverend expanded BANCO's activism. The group started picketing the St. Joseph courthouse every Tuesday. Pinkney carried a huge, wood-handled sign (he called it the Monster), which listed the judges' and other officials' names and labeled them as wanted criminals. One thing that marked BANCO's early efforts was their consistency; at least a few members of the core group would show up every Tuesday.

They also had a practice called "court watching," something the reverend does to this day. It consists of sitting in the courtroom during trials and hearings and making brief notes on the cases. These might include the case number, who was being charged, what the charges were and the results of the case.

Positive changes seemed to start taking place in the courtroom. Judges appeared to adhere more closely to the law now that they were being watched. Young men and women who thought they were being unfairly treated began to approach Pinkney and ask his advice. Cases that had previously been a cut-and-dried conviction were now being contested, with an occasional person holding out and resisting the pressures of pleading guilty. (Courts often have a tactic of tacking on additional charges with ridiculous amounts of jail time attached in order to get unknowing people to cave in and plead guilty to a "lesser" charge.)

The efforts of Pinkney and BANCO began to be noticed in the community; people saw them as fighters for justice and began to come to them for help. One day while he was court-watching, a woman named Belinda Brown approached the reverend and asked if she could have a few minutes of his time.

It seems her niece had been working for some time at the Eagle party store in Benton Harbor. She was a young, pretty girl and the owner was attracted to her. She resisted his advances, though, and apparently he didn't handle it very well. One day, when she turned him down, he became angry and slapped her, and then fired a round from his pistol into the wall. She called the police; they showed up and talked to the owner, but nothing further was done. According to Belinda, they didn't even make a police report!

When Pinkney heard the story, he decided to approach the very same prosecutor who had sent him to prison. He explained the situation and then said to him, "I expect you to prosecute this man." Perhaps the prosecutor was feeling guilty about his earlier action against Pinkney; he actually went after the store owner and the man ended up doing some time in jail. In the meantime, BANCO picketed the store and expressed so much displeasure at the store owner, the place had to close down.

Belinda's niece also hired a lawyer to sue the store manager and was awarded twelve thousand dollars (minus the lawyer's fees) in damages. None of this would have gotten off the ground if not for the help of BANCO and Rev. Pinkney, and the fledgling organization gained another loyal supporter.

It's a miracle anything happened at all, considering the wall of indifference most Benton Harbor residents face. They experience it in the media, in school, at their city commission meetings. The message is soundless, wordless and clueless, but they get it anyway. They don't count. And it's not just indifference; through lack of restraint, police are seemingly encouraged to create a climate of fear by intimidation. For example, the shortest route between the two cities is a bridge across the St. Joseph River, but most black people are afraid to go that way. "If they didn't have to cross that bridge, they wouldn't do it," says Pinkney, referring to most residents of Benton Harbor. "You couldn't pay them to do it."

Maintaining St. Joseph's de facto segregation policy requires police and judges to be, well, creative. "The government knows," says the reverend sadly. "They know how far to push these people. They know they can push these people close to the edge and they won't do anything, because they're so intimidated."

They pushed Terrence Shurn, literally, a little too far in the summer of 2003. He was sitting on his parked motorcycle on the side of the road on Empire St. near Pavone in Benton Harbor. Pinkney says a police officer approached from behind and nudged the cycle with his patrol car. Terrence, who was called T-shirt by almost everyone in town, tried to ignore the unprovoked attack on his person and property, but then the officer bumped him again. And again. Finally, pushed to the limit, Terrence took off on his bike, fast. The officer followed. What ensued was a high-speed chase through town, ending with the police forcing Terrence to crash into a building on his cycle. He was killed from the impact.

Understandably, the community was enraged. Many voices were raised in protest; even so, the people behaved with civility. A few nights after Terrence was killed, several neighbors and friends were holding a candlelight vigil for him, and the police came in and told them to break it up. The grieving group was already upset; their mood was volatile and this final blow set them off. They started hammering the officers with rocks and bottles. The police retreated and soon came back with reinforcements. By this time, the ugly mood had turned into mayhem, and people had started breaking things and setting fires.

Thus began the "uprising" in Benton Harbor, which was broadcast across the state and country, showing frightening images of burning buildings with hushed newscasters commenting about city-wide riots. In reality, the whole scene encompassed a couple of city blocks with not more than a dozen houses burned. Some suspect a few fires were set by unscrupulous landlords with hopes of collecting an insurance payoff. There were some injuries during the extended public reaction, but no one was killed.

Dignitaries like then-governor Jennifer Granholm and Jesse Jackson rushed in; Granholm dazzling with her brilliance and Jackson baffling with his charm. Impassioned speeches and grand promises were made (Pinkney says Granholm promised Benton Harbor its own courthouse), but nothing materialized in the way of benefits for the people of that besieged city.

In fact, things only seemed to be getting worse. Whirlpool, once the somewhat honest engine that drove the proud industrial town of Benton Harbor, now appeared poised to drain it of its last resources. On the burners at Whirlpool's development arm, Harbor Shores, was a sweet, multimillion dollar resort project topped off with a shiny new golf course designed by none other than the Golden Bear himself, Jack Nicklaus. The development was being sold to the people of Benton Harbor with the promise of jobs, jobs and more jobs being brought to the area. What wasn't revealed was that they would be low-paying service jobs, and not many at that. Sadly, the residents of Benton Harbor would again be smoothly left out, somehow sold out by an apparently bribed or clueless city commission. Harbor Shores would end up making a stupendous land grab, complete with infrastructure, in return for a pittance of jobs.

The reason the lie about the jobs had to be so good was that Harbor Shores required something from the citizens of Benton Harbor in order for the project to go through. It was a prime parcel of beachfront property in Jean Klock Park, the park itself bequeathed by the Klock family to the people of Benton Harbor "in perpetuity", which means forever. Acquiring the lakeshore was crucial to the Harbor Shores plan; it was to be the location of three magnificent tourist-drawing holes on Jack's golden green chem-treated expanse.

Harbor Shores, being a corporation, is legally known as a "person," so to speak, but could never be construed as "the people" by any stretch of the imagination. So, to make the dubious grab seem reasonable, the bigwigs at Whirlpool, Harbor Shores and other fine behemoths would have to do some, you know, maneuvering and stuff. All manner of fakes, feints, flummoxes, threats, cajolery, bribery, blackmail and other tricks from the well-worn bag would be on the table. If a certain pesky reverend couldn't keep his mouth shut, there were ways to deal with that. For now, though, it looked like smooth sailing, what with most of the important people already on board: representatives from Law, Philosophy, Religion, and of course, Real Estate. And if that city commission knew what was good for them, they'd go along, too.

6

Incredible Popeye Arms

I once ran for the city commission in Kalamazoo, along with two friends, Dennis Flatt and Charles Young. Dennis had given me the idea and then decided to run himself. He then encouraged Charles to join us, and we ran as a sort of team, pooling resources and sharing campaign literature. Charles, in his early twenties, soon realized he wasn't comfortable speaking in front of crowds but came to the candidate forums anyway. Dennis and I, both in our forties at the time, spoke quite freely; I had spent some time before audiences, and Dennis spoke about fathers' rights whenever and wherever he could.

I could fill a chapter with things I learned from that campaign, but two experiences stick out from the rest. Both occurred during the forums where candidates are expected to field questions and give their stance on issues. Dennis, articulate and intelligent, spoke eloquently on fathers' rights and other issues, but he had become cynical from the lack of open ears, and there was often a bitter tinge to his voice. Perhaps his bitterness offended some people, because at one forum, Dennis simply didn't show up, at least not until the speaking was over. He finally straggled in, looking pretty shaken up, with a gash over one eye. He never told us what happened, but we guessed he had been beaten up. His interest in the race declined and he would never talk about politics after that.

I remember another effective and far cleverer maneuver at one of the forums in a poor section of town. We felt we would have a lot of support in this crowd, seeing as we were the candidates for change. As we arrived, I noticed one of the incumbent candidates, a pretty blonde, chatting with a good/evil-looking man. The best analogy I can think of is the Reggie character from the old Archie comics. Anyway, when the event began, this Reggie guy got up and asked a question, with one condition: only the non-incumbent candidates were to answer. The question— about doing additional volunteer work—was innocent enough, but it had the effect of putting us newbies on the defensive, when the time probably could have been better spent airing grievances the public had with the current crew. It was a clever trap. Caught in our need to speak, to get our point across, we didn't see the maneuver for what it was and politely bowed to it. It wasn't much—just a subtle blind-side—but it was enough to take the wind out of our sails at an event where we could have made a decent splash.

In retrospect, perhaps we should have known we were out of our league. The chaste meeting rooms, full of sharp suits and careful hairdos cut to match, could have clued us in to the sacrosanct arena we were trying to enter. Politics seems to breed a certain animal: sensible, positive, practical, at home with Robert's Rules of Order, but somehow…lacking in some way. Or maybe it's not a lack at all, but an extra skin or something that wards off strong emotion and helps one slog through hours of bureaucratic sludge. From my experience, the casual visitor to a governmental meeting takes in the efficient half-smiles and is, perhaps, satisfied. He hears the muted voices carrying the special government tidbits and is probably impressed. He may also, however, feel a vague uneasiness; sense that he's somehow out of place, but it's not enough to make him miss dinner. More than likely, he'll ignore the vague red flag and tell himself that this is business better left to those who are obviously suited to it.

As we were to learn, this is the expected and desired reaction. Indeed, what the powers-that-be seem to want you, Joe or Jane Citizen, to do is to visit a meeting some time on your lunch hour or a field trip, feel the rush of participatory government, and then leave. If you must speak, please keep it under four minutes and then sit your ass down. (Please.) Next, please. And if you want to be elected...well, we learned something about that, too. A good analogy might be that we're all on the same ocean, but we're not on the same boat. The government, the insiders, have a boat all to themselves, and the only way for you to get on it is if they cast down their big Popeye arms and pull you aboard. It turns out the Popeye arms work both ways, and it wouldn't be long before we'd learn, through Pinkney, just how far the government would go to keep one of their own aboard.

It was 2004 and Edward Pinkney had now been in the Benton Harbor area more than ten years. As a reverend, he had spent the last four years picketing the Berrien County courthouse with members of BANCO every Tuesday and court-watching even more regularly than that.

His experiences had taught him to watch the movements of those in power, so he was aware of the plans for Harbor Shores, for instance, at an early stage. Expanding his territory, he began attending city commission meetings.

At the time, Glen Yarbrough and his brother, Charles, were both on the city commission, Charles in the role as mayor. But in Pinkney's opinion, Glen was the one in charge. "He was the muscle," says the reverend. "He would tell the others why they should vote a certain way, and normally they did."

Rev. Pinkney was for recalling Glen Yarbrough, but the others in BANCO weren't so sure. They thought that perhaps they should choose an easier target. Pinkney reasoned that outing a big fish like Yarbrough might scare the rest of the council members enough to get them to fall in line. The others agreed, and they decided to work toward Glen Yarbrough's recall.

So began the ingenious campaign that would foil the powers-that-be in Berrien County and temporarily depose a valuable corporate asset. However, the victory would be short and sweet, and punishment would soon follow. Heedless of consequences, Pinkney and BANCO began their recall work. They were aware of two major obstacles to victory: one, the formidable amount of resources Whirlpool could summon to suppress the effort if need be, and two, perhaps more importantly, the problem of getting voters to the polls. They decided to make the little-used absentee ballot their principal weapon in the election. Rev. Pinkney reminisced about the recall strategy in our 2013 interview. With light editing for clarity, here are a few of his comments:

Absentee voting is the best weapon you could ever come up with to win an election because most people really don't want to go to the polls. They always think about the long line... We went out and told them, and persuaded them, to vote absentee. We got every senior citizen that was available, every person who was planning to be out of town; we got every person who was handicapped. We got everybody who wanted to be part of it, and people wanted to be part of it.

When Pinkney mentions the elderly and handicapped, it's because they are among the apparently privileged few who can vote absentee, but there is a third category—those who plan to be "out of town." This provision is especially important because it contains the gray area that makes all government possible. Every restriction must have a loophole for the favored ones to pass through, and this one is easily traversed—after all, who's to say your travel plans can't change? Unfortunately, technicalities often only work for the well-connected; had the voters known about the midnight raids that were to follow the successful recall, they might not have been as keen to participate. But let's hear more from Pinkney:

On that day, that Monday, they got concerned, Yarbrough and his people. Then that Tuesday, the day of the election, they were worried, because we really didn't do any campaigning. We weren't hanging out at the polls; we weren't doing anything. All we did was wait, and then on

Election Day, we knew we had the lead—they had to catch up. He (Yarbrough) started panicking when he realized he was about to be recalled, and once he figured that out, he went to the sheriff's department.

At this point, Pinkney comments that the police found nothing amiss in the election, and they later testified to that in court, but here his account goes into realms that might stretch believability for those who haven't been touched by our justice system. He tells of police kicking down doors, including that of the city clerk, hiring seedy individuals as government witnesses, and finally, a judge wielding incredibly long Popeye arms.

As it turned out, Glen Yarbrough, city commissioner, shot down in a recall election by a score of 354 to 301, wasn't dead. Judge Paul Maloney raised him up, out of the reach of voters, and declared Glen Yarbrough a commissioner again. The reasons don't matter, the numbers don't match, but Judge Maloney, with all-powerful juris confidence, swiftly surmised the election was a fraud. (Such godly talents don't go unnoticed; Paul Maloney is now a federal judge at the district level.)

Shortly after the miraculous decision, the impeccable city clerk, Jean Nesbitt, was informally accused of somehow aiding BANCO's efforts and was relieved of her position. To Whom It May Concern, it looked as if this nasty recall business might go away quickly and cleanly—what with the voters nicely cowed, the city clerk smartly fired, and the election, of course, handily reversed. All that was needed now was to stay the course, keep the chin up…and get that pesky reverend out of the picture.

7

The Second Trial

We've now come almost full circle in our story to the time when I actually crossed paths with Rev. Pinkney, and then witnessed and filmed his first voter fraud trial. While Pinkney was plotting how to win an election, I was working on ways to start an online newspaper in Kalamazoo. I had put up a sign in a local café and soon had a group of ten or twelve volunteers who were willing to write for free. Others pitched in with story ideas or to set up the website. We'd meet Thursday evenings at the cramped, but cozy, Fourth Coast Café on Westnedge Avenue in Kalamazoo. The group varied from week to week, both in numbers and personalities. Discussions were usually lively, and meetings would often go into the late hours.

We were a naïve group, brimming with ideas and assuming we could handle all the details democratically. It would prove a difficult task. We started off well enough, and in a year's time, managed a small print edition and were hosting a show on local access TV. Morale was high at first, but mounting responsibilities with no pay started to become a problem. Petty arguments over minor matters started to creep in, too, wasting valuable meeting time. Then there was the problem of getting real news to fill the monthly edition; the majority of articles tended to be opinion pieces. As we were to learn, real reporting is time-consuming, often boring, and can be expensive, depending on the news item covered and the depth of research required.

All these issues would quickly lead to the demise of the *Kalamazoo Voice*, as we called ourselves, but not all was lost in the process. We experienced how organizations operate, and how they fail. We learned a little about group behavior and democracy (what works and what doesn't) and expanded our point of view from the endless ideas and stories that came out of those weekly gatherings. And we were left with a story that became more than just a news article, at least for me: an account revealing a justice system whose depth of corruption boggles the mind, and a man who could not stop telling his truth, no matter what the consequences.

I first heard Rev. Pinkney speak in May, 2005, at the Battle Creek, MI public library. My co-editor and I had driven the half hour from Kalamazoo with one of our staff writers, Kwame Shorter. (Shorter was a pen name.) Kwame was the one who had heard about Pinkney's role in helping the young men who were jailed naked, and it was he who found out that the reverend was going to speak.

We arrived to find him talking to a small group of maybe half a dozen in a large well-lit room near the front of the library. He was smiling and welcoming, and quickly filled us in on the recall, the reversal, and the political climate since. He wasn't pious like I thought a reverend should be—he was funny, actually, with a voice like Redd Foxx's. Besides humor and the voice, he seemed to share some of the comedian's scrappiness, too. He'd say things like, "We spanked 'em!" when referring to the commissioner's recall or any other victory. He seemed to revel in exposing hypocrisy and poked fun at it whenever he could. All officials, no matter what level, were targets of his biting humor. At the same time, his voice and eyes carried a gentleness that can only come from forgiveness. On some level, he seemed to genuinely like the people he was lambasting.

In between the humorous jabs, he told us a story about a community that had seen its share of loss—that of jobs, opportunity and quality of life, and loss of their children through a hungry justice system. In spite of all the cynicism this must have produced, they had still come together with enough political muster to oust a sitting commissioner. He told us about the funny math in the recall reversal, the firing of the city clerk shortly after, and the fact that the government was now coming after him. His humor was especially striking, considering the charges levelled against him carried a maximum term of twenty years in prison.

It all seemed a grave injustice, and we were anxious to cover his upcoming trial. Since we had experience with video cameras from doing our access show, he asked us to fill out a permission slip to film the trial. He mailed us the papers; we filled them out, mailed them back and the request was granted. In that way, we were able to film his first trial, which as you might recall, ended in a hung jury. Let's pick up the story from there.

The fact that ten jurors had bought the prosecutor's pseudo-case was disturbing, but two hadn't, and those in the Pinkney camp (where we now found ourselves) were elated, and the reverend declared it a victory. He was sure, though, that Berrien County would pursue the charges again, which in theory was permissible but hardly ever done in practice. Time would prove him right, as the Berrien County justice system would brush up on its game and properly repay the reverend for his insolence.

He had almost a year to prepare for his second trial, and in that time, some interesting things happened. His attorney, Tat Parish, told him he wouldn't be able to represent him a second time. For one thing, Pinkney couldn't afford him. The bill for the one trial and associated hearings was almost $40,000, an amount the reverend would be hard-pressed to pay. But more importantly, Mr. Parish probably felt he had done enough stepping on toes; he still had to work in that courthouse and rub elbows with the judges and prosecutors. So he let Rev. Pinkney go with a generous handshake, and settled the account for a mere $3000.

It wasn't like he was leaving the reverend stranded. Among others, Hugh "Buck" Davis, a highly experienced attorney in Detroit, had been following Pinkney's case and wanted to help. He offered to represent him *pro bono*. Davis then convinced his friend and colleague of almost forty years, Elliot Hall, to join in the effort. With the addition of Tim Holloway, Pinkney now had a formidable team of three attorneys working on his behalf.

The group would hit the ground running, presenting several motions dealing with prejudice by the court, the most important one criticizing how Berrien County picked its jury pools. The hours-long hearing resulting from this motion featured an expert who pointed out four specific ways that policies in this court eliminated minorities and poor people from jury pools. One technique, for instance, was to update prospective juror lists only once every four years, effectively eliminating those who had moved in that time period. There were three other equally damaging arguments, and I have a feeling the whole affair was an embarrassment to the court.

As it turned out, this would be the last time I was to have filming privileges in that courtroom. I had given all the footage from the first trial to a young filmmaker from Benton Harbor whose professional name was Steve Keys. With my co-direction, he had constructed an hour-long documentary on the trial called, *What's Going on in Benton Harbor?* The film, somewhat amateurish and at times with bad sound, nevertheless featured many of Tat Parish's excellent closing arguments and revealed the numerous gaps in the prosecution's case. A copy of the film somehow got into the judge's hands and he took exception to it, saying we had shown some of the jurors. What he was leaving out is that we had followed the court's instructions by standing behind the jury box, which should have taken care of things. But that didn't matter; Judge Butzbaugh ruled my camera out of the courtroom and that was the end of it.

Had the camera stayed in, it would have revealed the backs of twelve Caucasian heads in the jury box at the second trial. Out of a jury pool of seventy-five, only eight were African-Americans, and somehow all eight would end up being disqualified, leaving Rev. Pinkney, a black man, with a jury filled with all white peers. Some might call it a fluke, but the reverend says he peeked into an adjoining courtroom during a break from his own trial only to find the same scenario: a black person in the defendant's chair, with twelve white people in the judgment seats.

To be honest, I was somewhat relieved not to have the responsibility of filming the second go-round. The first trial had been a grueling three weeks of sitting through endless, seemingly senseless testimony, and waiting long days for a verdict that seemed like it would never come. Add to that a daily round trip of almost a hundred miles, and afterwards editing hours and hours of tape full of pointless testimony, and I was more than ready to give it up. There were practical matters, too, like a lack of money for gas and lunches, and the difficulty of getting time off work.

The upshot of all this is that I attended very little of the second trial and so can't give a first-hand account! Thank goodness for court reporting, though, because, for the price of a transcript, you can read almost everything that was said in that trial—even words the jury and audience were not allowed to hear. Rev. Pinkney managed to obtain a copy for less than four dollars a page, which sounds like a deal until you realize there were more than a thousand pages for a total cost of over five thousand dollars. Plus, the font size could almost qualify as large print, which reduces the amount of words per page, making it even more of a rip-off. Pinkney felt compelled to buy the transcript because he was told that it was absolutely necessary for an effective appeal. He says, though, if he hadn't received some inheritance money from his mother's death, he wouldn't have been able to afford it. The tall pile of typed testimony and legal lingo makes for boring reading, but there are a few highlights, some of which are presented here. With slight format changes, what follows is a faithful rendition of the court proceedings.

The first two selections both feature the prosecution's key witness, Brenda Fox. You might recall from the first trial that Brenda's testimony was tainted because it contradicted statements made a year earlier. Here being questioned by defense attorney, Elliot Hall, Ms. Fox is in typical form. Although she has gone over this in the past in court, right now she simply can't remember anything.

Hall: What did you tell the police when you—when they took a statement from you at the police station?

Fox: I can't exact—recall exactly what I told them.

H: You don't remember anything?

F: No.

H: About what you told the police?

F: Not exactly, no. You know how long it's been? You know, I really tried to get this out of my mind; to get it over with.

We feel you on that one, Brenda, though it seems things go more slowly when someone is fibbing. (The judge illustrates this exhaustively a little later on.) Today in court, the truth is a slippery thing, and Elliot Hall knows that asking Brenda Fox the same question twice could well produce two entirely different answers. Earlier in her testimony, Ms. Fox had stated that she registered to vote at age eighteen, and since then had voted pretty regularly. After some queries about the election, the soft-spoken attorney puts the question to her again, and poor Brenda contradicts herself so badly, Judge Butzbaugh has to lean in and help her out. Notice the court's pitiful plea just before Mr.Hall gracefully exits.

Hall: Have you voted in other elections...

Fox: No.

H: Ms. Fox?

F: No.

H: So you registered at the age of eighteen, is that correct?

F: (No verbal response)

H: To vote?

F: Yes.

H: And you have never voted in any election?

F: I have voted. I have voted. Correction. I have voted.

H: When was that, ma'am?

F: Lord have mercy.

Court: Just a minute.

Hall: Your Honor...

Fox: Know what? You is really...

H: (Inaudible)

F: ...you really—you better get next to me with these unnecessary...

H: Your Honor

F: ...questions.

Court: Mister—please.

Hall: Your Honor, I have no further questions.

It doesn't take a Rhodes Scholar to discern that either Brenda Fox is very confused, or something else is going on here. I spoke to one of Rev. Pinkney's attorneys, Buck Davis, on the phone in the fall of 2013. His voice has a soft Southern drawl, even though he's been practicing law in Detroit since 1968. Despite his Dixie roots, Davis was "stunned" at the apparent levels of racism that persist in the Berrien County courthouse, saying he's never been to a place that is so "overtly backward." In that kind of atmosphere, he says, "The black man's word means nothing."

He contends there was a kind of psychological warfare going on at the Pinkney trial. "There was a lot of police presence," he says, "and that intimidates a jury. They acted like the audience was a mob." He adds that the heightened security was hardly necessary, since the average age in the audience was probably around fifty.

Of course, some jury prospects were encouraged to stay out of the courtroom all together. Of the eight black people who made it into the jury pool, Davis maintains they were "...obviously terrified. They wanted to get off the jury." He surmised that some of the witnesses on the stand were under tremendous pressure, too. "They couldn't look up," he says. "They would freeze up, or cry."

It sounds like they've been through a lot, so let's excuse the jury and witnesses for now. They're not needed (or wanted) for this next segment anyway. It's a conversation that involves only members of the bar, that special lot who speak of law as "theories" that can be argued either way. At issue is a statement by a man named Mansell Williams that says Commissioner Yarbrough paid him ten dollars to say Pinkney bribed him to vote. The statement, if true, would undermine the entire investigation against Pinkney, since Glen Yarbrough's complaint started it all rolling. Mr. Hall has been questioning Yarbrough on the statement and Prosecutor Vigansky, for obvious reasons, objects. Ironically, this same piece of evidence was introduced before, at the first trial, by none other than Mr. Vigansky. Why he brought it in the first place is unclear, but now he has to fight to keep it out. He doesn't have to work too hard though—the judge has it covered for him.

Since the next section, like most court proceedings, runs on a little bit, try to have some fun with it. Count how many times the judge says the word, "relevant," or asks, "What difference does that make?" Feel Mr. Hall's frustration as he is forced to become ever more specific, or risk repeating himself, while his honor cleverly keeps him at bay. Cheer on Mr. Davis as he strives to bring some logic in at the end. And notice how it all comes to naught as the Butz stifles every offering into a neat little box of nothing. Extra Credit: Look up MRE 608(b) for me, because I'm sure not looking up the frigging thing.

We'll pick up this conversation in the middle—it doesn't really matter—everything has to be endlessly repeated anyway, because "the court" is playing hard to get and refuses to understand. Don't, however, confuse his stubbornness with battiness; Judge Butzbaugh is a former president of the state bar and knows what he is doing.

Well, here goes, put your waders on. Note the abbreviations after each participant speaks their first line. Judge Butzbaugh has been abbreviated twice because of his special status.

Butz: Mr. Hall, let me—let's just jump to a conclusion that...

Hall: Yes.

B: ...everything that Mansell Williams says is true.

Hall: All right.

Butz: I mean—just—just—I'm not saying it is, but just to—to carry on our discussion here. What difference does that make as to whether the Defendant is or is not guilty in this charge?

H: Because it goes to the—it has an impact on the prosecution's case in terms of the prosecuting—Prosecutor pointing to the Defendant saying that he paid five dollars for people to vote. And Mansell—Mansell Williams indicated that was not the case, Your Honor.

B: So—so, if—if the—if the Prosecutor improperly charged the Defendant...

H: Yeah.

B: ...the jury should find him "not guilty."

H: That's correct. That's why it's...

B: What does that have to do with whether—what—what Mr. Yarbrough did or did not do?

H: Your Honor, I think it has an impact on his motive when he went to the Prosecutor's Office.

B: What difference does it make what his motives were?

Hall: Because it started—it started the investigation that caught—landed the Defendant in Court, Your Honor.

Butz: What difference does that make? We're—we're here on a trial...

H: Now that it's being offered...

B: Just a moment. We're here—just a moment. We're here on a trial...

H: Yes.

B: ...alleging that—that the Defendant did certain specific things. What somebody's motive was in pointing the finger at the Defendant and—and instituting or initiating the investigation, what difference does that make?

H: Your Honor, I think I made—I can't be more exhaustive than I've already been.

B: Well, I—I—you haven't got me convinced because I don't understand it.

H: Well, I—you don't understand it, then I got nothing further to say to the Court.

B: Okay.

It appears the veteran attorney is down, but Mr. Hall is not giving up yet. He knows that even if he doesn't win this round, if the judge contradicts his own, earlier ruling, that reversal could be grounds for an appeal.

Hall: All I can say is, you admitted it at the last trial. If you want to...

Butz: But...

H: ...make a different ruling...

B: Well, I'm trying...

H: ...that's up to you.

Let's give Judge Butzbaugh a minute to gather his wits and come up with an answer. Meanwhile, note how Prosecutor Vigansky labels everyone who gets on the stand a Defendant, whether it be a commissioner, the mayor or the former city clerk. Also, perhaps more importantly, Mr. Vigansky said that he did something.

Butz: Well, I'm trying to figure out why it was admitted the last time and Mr. Vigansky said that he did something. And I'm not—I don't—I do not remember. But Mr. Vigansky, can you tell me how that—what—how that came about the last time?

Vigansky: Yeah. The Defendant that was testifying on the stand...

Butz: Who was testifying?

Vigansky: I believe it was Ms. Nesbitt or Ms. Harper or maybe even Mr. Cook about that particular—let me think...

B: Well—I mean—if we have to...

Hall: I—I would be more...

B: ...we'll stop and take—we'll stop—stop the whole trial and go over this doggone thing. It's disturbing to me that this is coming up at this point. I have given you—given everybody every opportunity to bring this on so we can move this trial along and give the jury a chance to get to—to—to resolve this thing.

V: I brought it up...

B: And...

V: ...for impeachment purposes, Your Honor. It was through their witnesses. It was...

B: Did they object?

V: No, they wanted it in there. But it was for...

B: So...

Vigansky: ...impeachment...

Butz: But who were you impeaching?

V: I believe it was Ms. Nesbitt. Why she would have typed something up out of her office. It's clearly an extension...

B: Well—I—Mr. Hall, I will tell you, I—I do not understand how this can be relevant in this case, but I'm going to give you an opportunity, and if takes getting out that transcript and reading it, that's what we're gonna do. So, who's got the transcript?

At this point, all the litigators locate their copy of the transcript and find the correct page.

Butz: Did Mansell Williams testify at the first trial?

Vigansky: No.

Butz: Okay, well, the—looking at pages 731 to 733, the Prosecutor offered into evidence, "The Defendant said that he had no objection to its being received and that he was going to ask Mayor Cook about it. That he withdrew any objection." So that's an entirely different setting than what we have here today where there is an objection. Now, Mr. Vigansky, in the first trial, it looks like that you asked Ms. Nesbitt questions about that.

V: I did.

Butz: And are you planning to ask anybody questions about this exhibit?

Vigansky: Not if it's not coming in. I'm not bringing it up. Especially, since Ms. Nesbitt, I don't believe, is going to testify.

B: I don't know why it was—you know—what the motivation was to do it the last time, but it was offered by the Prosecutor; the Defendant did not object, and so I admitted it. And that's the reason it came in.

Hall: Well Your Honor, there is a line of evidence. We have several people involved with this—this Exhibit, Your Honor. We've got the mayor of Benton Harbor involved. We've got a Commissioner at Large, Etta Harper, involved. She was—originally took the report of Mansell Williams and she turned it over to the Mayor. The Mayor then asked the Clerk, Jean Nesbitt, to transcribe it, and then he gave a copy of it to the police department. So, I—this is—because it came in through Ms. Nesbitt, is the Court saying that because she is not testifying, it cannot come in?

B: No. What I'm saying is I don't understand the relevance to begin with. I—I—forgetting the hearsay issue, we are not gonna—we are not trying this case over something that someone else allegedly did in this—in this election. We're trying this case over what the Defendant allegedly did.

Hall: All right.

Butz: And I do not understand what any allegation of what Mr. Yarbrough did or did not do—what relevance that has in this litigation.

H: Well, because he—he—well, Your Honor, I've put my position on the record and...

B: That it relates to—to the initiation of the investigation is what...

H: That is correct.

B: ...I've understood you to say.

H: And—and also bias on the part of the witness in terms of...

B: Okay.

H: ...pointing to the Defendant.

B: In the initiation of the investigation, you're saying?

H: Yes, Your Honor.

Butz: Okay. Well, I—I do not understand how that can be relevant as to what this Defendant did or did not do leading up to this election.

Hall: Well, as I've indicated, Your Honor, I'm—we're not asking for this for the truth of the matter, but the effect it's going to have on the future witnesses. But I'm going to ask Ms. Harper and Mr. Cook about it.

Butz: Well, what are you going to ask them of it? What could they—you're going to ask them about that statement?

H: That is correct, Your Honor.

B: And what—if it's not relevant—what is the significance of it?

H: Is it the Court's position that it's not relevant at all to these proceedings?

Touché, Mr. Hall, and well done, but watch how the robed wonder sidesteps it.

B: Well, I haven't figured out yet its relevance.

H: Well, when those witnesses...

B: Well, your...

H: When those witnesses are presented, Your Honor, particularly, Etta Harper, she will indicate that Mansell Williams contacted her about this and...

Butz: Is this after the election?

Hall: This is after the election, Your Honor.

B: Okay.

H: And that the tape was then made pursuant to the request of the Mayor. She gave the tape to the Mayor. The Mayor made a business record of it by having the clerk transcribe it and making it a part of Benton Harbor records and giving a copy over to the Prosecutor as part of this whole investigation.

B: Okay.

H: So, it's a business record of—of the County.

B: But what difference does that make?

H: It has an impact upon how—again, Your Honor, how this investigation got started and the fact that...

B: But what difference does it make how the investigation got started?

H: Your Honor, it has especially—it has an—an impact based on the principal party who started the investigation. Mr. Yarbrough—he's the center of this, Your Honor.

B: Mr. Yarbrough has, so far as I can tell, and listening to the testimony in this trial, has absolutely nothing to do with what—whether the Defendant did or not do the acts with which he's charged.

H: Your Honor, this case would not have been started if the Defendant had—if the witness had not complained about the election. He is the—he started...

B: What difference does that make?

H: ...the investigation.

Butz: What difference...

Hall: So, he had a—he had a motive, Your Honor.

Let's ring the bell a minute and give Mr. Hall a virtual break. He's been punching away at the court while the judge covers up with both gloves; on the left His Honor wears "That's not relevant," and on the right, "What difference does that make?" This will continue until Elliot Hall exhausts all avenues of argument, and Buck Davis has to step in and help. Speaking of exhaustion, I imagine you're feeling that way—I know I am—but let's try and get through this, because at the end, the judge does some pretty good talking, or something. Anyway—ding.

Butz: Okay, but let's assume he has a motive. What difference does Mr. Yarbrough's motive have to do with whether the Defendant did or did not do what he's charged with?

Hall: Well, Your Honor, I think I've made it rather clear as if—he was if—Mr. Yarbrough did not—if he had not said that Reverend Pinkney was paying people five dollars, this—this case would not be in this courtroom.

Butz: But that doesn't mean that he did or did not do the acts with which he is charged.

H: Yeah, well I've asked him about whether he (inaudible) can say "yes" or "no."

B: You've asked him whether what?

H: If I—if I—I've asked him whether or not he paid Mansell Williams ten dollars to say that Reverend Pinkney paid five dollars to another voter. He can say "yes" or "no."

B: Well—and he said, "No." He's already testified the answer is "No."

H: All right. Is that—is the Court saying I can ask him that—that—that...

B: Well, you've asked him...

H: ...answer stays on the record?

That's a good point, Mr. Hall. Should we even have to ask that question? Let's see how Mr. Vigansky feels and then let the court take over.

Butz: Just a moment. Mr. Vigansky, on that particular issue, what is your position?

Vigansky: It's still hearsay. He's using an out of court statement. He's impeaching, basically, his own witness.

Butz: Well, I will tell you, the only theory I can come up with is one with which Mr. Davis disagrees with me as to the law, and that's under MRE 608(b). And under that theory, if it relates to the truthfulness or untruthfulness of the witness, you could ask the question. It might have something to do with the truthfulness or untruthfulness of Mr. Yarbrough. That's the only theory that I can come up with as we are sitting here talking about this, as to why—as to how you could possibly ask the question. You've asked the question. You've already got an answer, but let's set that aside for a second. Mr. Vigansky, you're standing. I assume you want to say something.

Mr. Vigansky does say something, but let's set that aside as well. He's a minor player in this volley and doesn't have a big enough gun to do the job. Your Honor…

Butz: Just a moment. I don't think that's quite right. The question to be asked—there has to be a good faith basis for asking the question. You do have something in writing.

But under 608(b) you—you are prohibited from presenting any extrinsic evidence about by it, which means that—that you cannot present the Mayor, you cannot present Ms. Nesbitt, or anyone—anyone else to—regarding that. Your—whatever—whatever the Defendant—whatever Mr. Yarbrough says is the end of it.

Hall: I...

Butz: So that's—that's the way I understand MRE 608(b).

H: So is the Court indicating that if the Mayor comes in and Etta Harper comes in, this—this evidence cannot come in...

B: That...

H: ...unless—unless Mansell Williams comes here and testifies?

Well, under 608(b)—my understanding of it anyway—I've forgotten why, but it had something to do with somebody doing something, and no, I would say, not even then.

Butz: Well, not—not even Mansell Williams. My understanding of MRE 608(b), as—as I have—I've forgotten the issue now, but we ruled on it earlier in this case, something to do with something the Defendant said—a question that Mr. Vigansky asked the Defendant and Mr. Davis made a motion in limine objecting to that and I overruled that on this very point. That's the only theory that I can come up with, as I'm sitting here, as to how you could ask him anything about this. In my view, it has absolutely no relevance to this trial. If something like this can come in, trials would—would never be able to move forward because there would always be something about "somebody did this" or "somebody did that" to influence an investigation or to start an investigation or something. The—the issue here is what the Defendant did or did not do as alleged by the Prosecutor. What Mr. Yarbrough did or did not do in initiating the investigation has nothing to do with what the Defendant did.

Hall: Then, Your Honor, is the Court indicating that during the course of the first trial, it should not have come in even during Ms. Nesbitt...

Butz: Well, it wasn't—if—if it had been presented to me for the purpose of—with an objection, I don't see where my ruling would have been any different than it is today. But the Defendant—but the Prosecutor offered it, the Defendant read it, and I think the Defendant's attorney decided he wanted it in, too.

H: That's correct.

B: And so they both agreed and so I let it in.

H: So, it's the Court's position now that since it's being contested, under your understanding of the rules of evidence, it's—it's not appropriate. Is that...

B: I do not see where—well, number one, I do not see where it's relevant. I mean—that's the number one issue. The second issue is, it is hearsay, obviously. Without ruling on a hearsay issue—I mean—there might be some—some way to have—to do something about the hearsay issue, I—but I'm not going to try to work our way through that at this point. I don't see any need to. I do not see what— where—what Mr. Yarbrough did or did not do, after this is over, what that has to do with—with the relevant—the relevant issues in this litigation. Now, Mr. Davis...

At this point, Buck Davis gets up to speak and is told to get back by the court recorder. This won't be the last time he will be told to keep his place. Poor Mr. Davis—if only he had brought along his proper authority, his argument might not be falling on deaf ears.

Davis: I'm sorry. It seems to me, Your Honor, that it's relevant, not necessarily for the truth, or whether or not it became an official record of the city when the Mayor told the clerk to transcribe it. I specifically asked (Detective) Dannaffel, when he was presented by the Prosecutor,

"Did you become aware of this allegation?"
"Yes."

"Did you investigate it?"
"No."

A part of the defense of this case has been our attack on the integrity of the investigation; the manner in which it was initiated, and the manner in which it was carried out, and the manner in which the matter has gone forward for the last two years. According the testimony of the Mayor, when he became aware of this tape, which was made by a commissioner, a woman of equal stature to—it was volunteered to Etta Harper, a commissioner just like Yarbrough is, she recorded it, then she played it for the Mayor, and then the Mayor directed the clerk to transcribe it. According to the Mayor, he turned it over to the police. But that aspect of the case, according to Dannaffel, he didn't know about and he didn't do anything.

Butz: Let—let me just stop you for a second.

Davis: Okay.

B: Where is that statement?

D: I'm sorry?

B: I want to look at that statement.

D: I don't have it.

Butz: Just a moment. Stay right where you are. Mr. Davis, don't—go right back to—Mr. Davis?

Davis: I'm sorry. Back there?

B: Let's just assume that it's true—this is an assumption that Mr. Yarbrough paid ten dollars to say that Pinkney—that the Defendant paid him something.

D: Correct.

B: Does that change what the Defendant did or did not do?

D: Well, obviously, nothing can change what the Defendant did or didn't do.

B: That's the point.

D: Okay.

B: That does not change. We're here as to what the Defendant did or did not do. Let's just say that the Prosecutor said, "Okay." "I'm—I'm going to prosecute both of them."

D: Right. But the...

B: But what difference would it make?

D: The...

Butz: This case stands or falls on the merits of this case.

Davis: The intimidation or interest of any given witness or person involved in the process, it seems to me, is a part of the case. Just like...

B: Well...

D: ...our claim...

B: All right.

D: ...that witness after witness has either been intimidated or else had some guilty or other untoward interest. Now when Dannaffel says, "Yes, I became aware of this fact and I didn't investigate it." It seems to me, Your Honor, that goes to the integrity just like, "Did you do this, did you do this, did you do fingerprints, did you...?" Therefore, it doesn't have to be accepted for the purpose of the truth or non-truth; it goes to the integrity of the prosecution.

B: But Mr. Davis, do you have some authority that that is proper?

D: I'm sorry?

B: Do you have some legal authority that I can look at that is proper?

Vigansky: Your Honor?

Davis: ...that—we both assumed that because there was no objection last time that we'd be dealing with it straightforwardly this time.

Hall: But if the Court wants some authority, we would—we would certainly present it, Your Honor.

The Butz: Okay. Well, I'm going to need something because at this point this case is about this case and it's about the evidence that was presented in it. It's not about some other charge that—that may or may not or should or should not have been brought against a different individual that is not related to what the Defendant did. So, I—if you want time to—to research, I'm certainly willing to do that. And if you want to proceed without—I don't know.

Thank you, Your Honor; we're tired now. Besides, further research will probably show that it would be easier for a camel to get through the eye of a needle, than for Mr. Williams' statement to get back in this courtroom.

Why don't we move on to the conviction then, and quickly, so we can end this chapter. If my recollection is correct, the jury took three and a half days to deliberate in the first trial, whereas this time, Rev. Pinkney says, it was "like they went out on a cigarette break" before pronouncing him guilty of crimes worth twenty years in prison.

8

The Buck Naked Fish

Being locked up right away might have given the reverend a kind of hero status; that's probably why he was sentenced to house arrest for a year on an electronic tether. Strangely, being cooped up never seemed to bother him, and he was soon lost in a flurry of activity. He couldn't travel but he could talk, and in no time was hosting his own weekly internet talk radio show, something he does to this day. He spent endless hours on the phone networking and planning strategies and taking time to listen to those who were caught in the tangled web of the justice system.

He continued to write as well; scathing articles that exposed the underhanded court and corporate dealings in the Benton Harbor area. One article severely criticizing Judge Butzbaugh appeared in a Chicago-based paper called the *People's Tribune*. It was this opinion piece that would again put him behind prison walls. In the article, he quoted a passage from the Bible saying, in effect, that God was going to get the judge for his dishonesty. Somehow, Judge Butzbaugh saw the words as a threat on his life, and again the police showed up at Pinkney's door.

He was brought before Judge Dennis Wiley, who appears to be a questionable student of jurisprudence at best. The judge quipped that Rev. Pinkney enjoyed a "direct line to God" and therefore posed a serious threat. Judge Wiley deemed Pinkney's article a probation violation and sentenced the reverend to a year in prison.

For Pinkney supporters, the months of house arrest had been a kind of limbo, with the court ready and waiting for the reverend to trip up. It would be rather difficult to not stumble; his probation restrictions ran three pages long. Unbelievably, there was even a provision forbidding him to go to church! It appeared to be a custom-made list designed to help the reverend fail, so his going to prison seemed like a foregone conclusion. Even so, when he finally did go, it hit like a dull blow to the gut; I felt blind-sided and began to suspect that fighting was useless. The enemy was too persistent, too powerful and too all-encompassing to be reckoned with. I felt myself crawling into a mental cocoon and forgot about activism for a while.

Activism is tough going anyway; it can be boring, time-consuming and uncomfortable, and there is usually a cross section of people who don't like you. Most demonstrations are held outside, so if the weather is bad, that's another strike against you. Even if the day is nice, walking in a picket line can feel trite or embarrassing, and repeated slogans grow silly quickly. And there is nothing like the threat of losing your job to shake a protester's confidence, or police standing ready to arrest you. Perhaps most disheartening is to simply be ignored—to expend all that effort and not a damn thing changes.

Now it looked like the strongest fighter I knew had been knocked out and wouldn't be getting up for a while.

Despite having a veritable team of lawyers, my activist champion appeared to have been silenced.

I couldn't have been more wrong. Rev. Pinkney appears not only to have survived prison, but thrived and flourished doing what he does best: bringing people together. In fact, he would prove to be so successful at this, the prison system would be at a loss as to what to do with him.

The first stop was Jackson Prison, where routine matters like a physical and blood tests were taken care of. His biggest complaint was how bad the food was and says he ate very little of it, sticking mostly to fruits and juices when he could get them. He tells about an inmate who would make him something called a "cook-up" every Saturday. When he described how it was made, I almost gagged, but he said it was about the best thing he could get in there.

On the fifth day of his confinement, several things happened. First, he was visited by two of his lawyers, Tim Holloway and Buck Davis, who told him the American Civil Liberties Union (ACLU) was interested in taking his case. They urged him to work with the national organization, whose name and resources would go a long way toward gaining his freedom. Pinkney figured that Davis, Hall and Holloway should handle the case; they had done a lot of work and they deserved the credit, he thought. Later in the day, three lawyers from the ACLU came to call and asked Rev. Pinkney to let them represent him. He hesitated, and then told the attorneys to talk it over with Davis and the others, and he would abide by their decision. Sometime after that, Buck Davis visited Pinkney again and told him the ACLU would be handling his appeal.

Pinkney received one more unexpected visitor that day, a woman representing the Green Party. She asked if the reverend would run as their candidate for U.S. Congress. He pointed out that he couldn't very well campaign from prison, but she assured him that just being there would get him some votes, and it would take his political fight to a new level, since his opponent would be none other than Republican Fred Upton from Whirlpool's founding family. Sadly another favorite, Democrat Don Cooney from Kalamazoo, would also run in this race. The campaign would turn out to be largely symbolic for Rev. Pinkney since Cooney would end up taking most of the anti-Upton vote. Still, the Green party's recognition gave a tremendous boost to the reverend's credibility.

All of these high-powered visits were announced over the prison loudspeaker, so by the end of the day, virtually everyone in Jackson Prison knew who he was and why he was there. He was getting publicity on the outside, too, with frequent news blurbs and a supportive article from the Detroit-based paper, the *Michigan Citizen*. His story even made Bill O'Reilly's show, though he wasn't cast in a favorable light. He was shown in a prison uniform with the controversial host wondering why a preacher would find it necessary to fight for justice in America! Mr. O'Reilly's insanely pat observations, as usual, didn't warrant a reply.

After twenty-nine days in Jackson, Pinkney was sent to Hiawatha, a low-security prison in Michigan's Upper Peninsula. For unknown reasons, he was transported about a week later to the far west side of the peninsula, a sixteen hour drive from Benton Harbor, to a prison called Ojibway. It was here that he would make his indelible mark, engineering a political action that would make prison officials scramble to keep up. In the process, he would bring together one of the most rigidly divided populations known, and he would make it all happen in less than a week.

Rev. Pinkney can't talk about his stay at Ojibway Prison without telling the story of the Buck Naked Fish, which is what the following episode has come to be called. If you detect a note of pride in his voice, it is well deserved; sometimes the reverend is so good, he even impresses himself. With brief interruptions and light editing, here are some of his thoughts on that adventure.

> I get there and the first guy I run into was this Muslim brother. He was about six-foot-five, talked more or less in riddles, but he wanted—he needed help. He said, "Reverend Pinkney! What you going to do to help us?" (I'm thinking) Help y'all? You know. Here I am, standing a nickel over five-seven, and here you is asking me what I'm going to do to help you. You about six-five, six-six. That didn't make no sense. And he had about five hundred Muslim brothers…I really had no idea what to do.

But he would take steps anyway while a plan formed in his mind. After he talked to the Muslim brother, he approached a man who made it a rule not to talk to black people—the leader of a group called the Aryan Nation.

> I asked him could I speak with him, and he said, "You must be new here. You know I don't talk to

black people." And I said, "Well, that's not really important right now." I said, "You don't have to like me. As a matter of fact, you don't ever have to talk to me again. But we got a problem, and we need your help; and you got a problem, and you need my help." He looked at me like he was wondering, "Who is this guy?" We must have just stood there and looked at each other for at least a couple of minutes. Then I said, "You wanna walk?" and we started walking around the field, and everybody could see me and him walking and talking. Everybody: the Muslim brothers, all of them; everybody saw it, and it was incredible. This guy was a big dude, you know, he was BIG, and rangy, and didn't like black people. And we just started talking. I told him why I was there; I explained that I had quoted a Scripture from Deuteronomy 28, starting with the fifteenth verse, and they threw me in jail. "I fight," I said, "I fight everything." I told him there was never a fight I didn't like. If there was a fight, I would be right there in the middle of it. So we kept walking; we probably did maybe ten rounds around this field. Two rounds is a mile, so we walked and talked for about, I would say, two hours or more. And at the end of the conversation, I said, "I'd like for you to be a part of what we're trying to do here. We've got to do something." I said I hadn't thought yet of what we were going to do, but I was leaning toward a food strike. He told me, "I can't give you a decision right now; I've got to go back and talk to my people. But some time tomorrow, we'll talk." This man had never, ever spoken to black people… and what that did, it opened up something for them to start communicating. I can't say for the other guys; they spoke to black people, but they didn't do it around him. So he went and spoke to his people…the only information he had was that there was going to be a food strike, and I think that got him excited, that somebody finally came there that wanted to do something. So then I went and had a talk with the Skinheads…

His powwow with the Aryan Nation leader had seemed to break the ice, and soon the leader of the Skinheads was on board. Pinkney kept moving, targeting leaders of all the different subgroups that exist in every prison.

I went and got the Mexicans, the Puerto Ricans, the Baptists…and finally, by the end of the day, we had more than a thousand people that were willing to join. By the leaders—I went after the leaders, not the individuals because the leaders run their unit. I don't care what prison you go to; the Mexicans, they have their leaders, the Skinheads have their leaders, the Muslim brothers have their leaders. Everybody has a leader inside the prison system. Then you got these young boys that just don't do nothing; I really didn't mess with them because they didn't really have a leader. If they wanted to join, it was okay with me, but we knew what we had; we had one thousand, about, one hundred and some, and it was fourteen hundred people in the whole complex. So, we didn't get everybody, but we got more than eighty per cent of them…

Now the reverend had to come up with a plan. Someone had mentioned a particularly bad tasting item on the prison menu—the Buck Naked Fish.

I had never seen it, I had never had the opportunity to smell it, but I'm going by what people are saying, that it was the nastiest, smelliest fish you can imagine…they only cooked one hundred pieces, and you're talking about fourteen hundred people on this complex; you know it must be real bad. So we chose the Buck Naked Fish. And it was so dramatic because they go by housing units: A, B, C, D, E, F, G—they started with A. There's a hundred and forty people in A. They only cooked a hundred pieces of the Buck Naked Fish so we got over a hundred of them just to go ask for the fish. They ran out after unit A but they didn't see the thing; they thought it was just a coincidence. Unit B goes and asks for the Buck Naked Fish and they don't have any more, so now they're giving them peanut butter and jelly sandwiches. One thing about when you're in prison, whatever is on that menu, that's what you have to serve to people. They have a substitute, because everybody doesn't want to eat the fish. What they usually have is peanut butter and jelly. So everybody came and asked for the peanut butter and jelly in unit B, and they ran out of peanut butter and jelly...

They called in the warden. This is on a Saturday; he doesn't work on Saturdays. He calls in his lieutenants and everybody else. They're thinking it's about to be a riot, an uprising, because this has never happened before... something was going on—they didn't know what it was. They had extra guards there, and they had police officers outside the fence.

Here's what made it so good; they didn't know who was behind it...they knew it wasn't me (!) because I had just got there that week. I got there Tuesday, and it was Saturday when we pulled it off. It was good because you saw a whole lot of different people working together. Doing something like this was so powerful; even the warden couldn't figure out what happened or who did it. So now, the next week, what they're going to do, they're going to outsmart us. They're going to do something entirely different; entirely new. They're going to cook eight hundred pieces of the Buck Naked Fish...we had a guy inside the kitchen, and he gave us the word; he said, "They're cooking 800 pieces!" We already knew what we were going to do, but we didn't tell him. We had all decided we were not going to go; we were not going to eat at all that day. So everybody is just sitting around; nobody is going to lunch. And you could smell the fish. You cook a hundred pieces, you could smell it. But can you imagine eight hundred pieces? Of course, they always had their regulars, the ones who eat the Buck Naked Fish, but other than that, nobody was going in there. And at the end of the day, the warden was there, and he was mad. He's trying to figure out, "Who is this guy?" or "Who is doing this?" You know, it can't be me! That Monday or Tuesday, I don't know what day it was, I was talking to Dorothy on the phone and the next thing I know, they had about six guards coming to get me, and telling me that, "You outta here!" I had to go pack my bags then and there, and they put me on a bus to Marquette.

So ended the saga of the Buck Naked Fish, but its effects would linger on long after. Pinkney says people still talk about it, amazed that something like that could be pulled off in the ultra-controlled atmosphere of a prison.

His action would earn him the unique status of "undesirable" in the Michigan prison system. An offhand remark about the lack of a microwave would be enough to send him packing from Marquette, and he would then be passed around the prison system like a hot potato, making a total of ten stops in less than five months.

Again and again, prison wardens would show themselves unable to stand up to the challenge of this unexpected champion, this streetwise reverend with a genius for organizing. At one institution, he would even be told, "We don't want your kind here!" One has to wonder exactly who they *do* want in prison—certainly not someone with enough personal magnetism to unite a widely diverse and disparate population.

It appears that, to prison officials, what Rev. Pinkney had done was unforgiveable, intolerable and a threat to systems of control everywhere. At the same time, it gave fourteen hundred prisoners a close-up look at the unequaled power of a united populace. It turned one man completely around: the leader of the Aryan Nation contacted Rev. Pinkney after his release, and they have since become phone buddies.

His merry-go-round tour of Michigan prisons would end with a three-week stay at a prison in Traverse City, at which time the ACLU would obtain an appeal bond for his release, getting him home in plenty of time for Christmas. The ACLU would enlist the help of several heavy hitters, including the Catholic Church, to write briefs on his behalf. The appeal court ended up reversing Judge Wiley's ruling, and on December 14, 2008, Rev. Pinkney walked out of the courtroom a free man.

9

Betrayal and the Status Quo

Betrayal tends to invoke the most visceral of human emotions. Whether it comes from a parent, a lover, a cherished group that one belongs to, or even oneself, it seems to reach down to the depths of our heart and demand harsh payment.

A friend of mine, I'll call him Jim Mason, once told me a story. He was eligible for the draft during the Vietnam War, and in July of 1969, he was one rider on a busload of boy-men, some of them he knew, coming from the west side of the state to Fort Wayne in Detroit. Before long, they were sitting in an amphitheater with hundreds of other potential draftees taking part in pre-induction testing. Included with the test materials was a sheet of paper that Mason said contained "scores" of organizations that the military considered subversive. He raised his hand and asked if the SDS was considered a subversive organization. He was talking about the Students for a Democratic Society chapter on the campus at Western Michigan University. The organization was leading anti-war protests, but Jim didn't really go along with their ideology; at that time, he believed in the war in Vietnam. His main goal by going to meetings was to get close to a coed he found attractive.

Little did he know, though, with that question, he went from potential draftee to criminal suspect.

They got him when he was waiting for his physical, standing in his underwear with the rest of his belongings in a brown paper bag, following a yellow line from checkpoint to checkpoint. Almost before he could say "Constitution," he was sidestepped out of line by two military policemen who proceeded to march him down a street with heavy traffic, still clad in his underwear and carrying his brown bag of belongings.

They brought him to the Fort Wayne administration building and locked him in an interrogation room. He says the small, windowless room was just like in the movies, complete with a single light bulb hanging from the ceiling. The weather was hot, in the nineties, and he sat there in his underwear, sweating. An interminably long wait, and then more surreality: a stereotypical federal agent dressed in a trench coat and fedora, not appearing to sweat, and armed with photos from SDS meetings. Some of the scenes looked familiar, and Jim realized he had been at some of those meetings. He was struck by an eerie feeling and realized instantly what most of us are just waking up to recently: the government has eyes and ears everywhere. They are at least as close as the local university, and more than likely, are much closer. Nowadays, they're probably right in the living room—you might never know until the photographs.

Mason told the guy what he knew, pointed out the girl he liked in a photograph, and was left to wait again until the guards finally came and escorted him back the way he had come. He was placed back in line where he had left it, only much further behind the others he had ridden out with. When he finally got out to the parking lot, three busloads of angry young men sat waiting in the sweltering heat, confined to metal buses without air conditioning. They had finished their tasks three and a half hours before, and everyone knew that it was Jim Mason who was holding them up. Somehow the word "traitor" got attached to his name and those men-boys—even some that he knew—beat the crap out of him all the way home, so badly that some of his teeth were loosened.

"That woke me up" says Mason now, when he talks about it. "It was an object lesson. They are the worst people in the world; they'll do whatever they want to get what they want. I told them that they had me wrong. I was a trained, lifelong, evangelical Christian, conservative Republican. Up to that point, I had thought what we were doing in Vietnam was right, but it was this Kafkaesque scene they produced that changed me forever."

What distinguishes Mr. Mason and Rev. Pinkney is that each started out believing that the system is fair and working, until they were handed overwhelming evidence that it is not. Both men seemingly have, like in the Matrix, taken the red pill and started the journey down the awful rabbit hole. For Mason, this has meant endless hours of internet research, followed by emails to a wide circle of friends and associates, bringing them up to snuff on clues he's found. Nonetheless, he feels his efforts have been mostly fruitless and that the majority of Americans are still unaware that their government is lying to them.

Rev. Pinkney's experiences have made him cynical, too. Still, he thought he could count on that stalwart organization, the NAACP. Unfortunately, time would show that the National Association for the

Advancement of Colored People, like just about everybody else, bows to political and economic pressure.

He started his relationship with the NAACP in his characteristic way, literally resurrecting the Benton Harbor chapter and running for its president. He enlisted the help of his growing network of supporters, generating a membership of over three hundred, which won the election easily. I was one who voted for the reverend and also served as a vote verifier for his side. I remember the preciseness of the voting procedure and how everything was counted and double-checked. That's why it was puzzling when the national organization came back a couple of years later and tried to contest his right to the office.

For now, he was off and running, using the clout of the NAACP to beef up his already-existing programs and to help create new opportunities. It appeared to be a union made in heaven. Voted most active in the state, his chapter would garner seven awards in just the first year. Their work in court watching was praised and recognized and the idea spread to other chapters around the country. It was when he instituted the boycott of all Whirlpool products that it became time for the reverend to go, but the marriage would sour long before that. One of the local chapter's first actions was to march in protest against the newly installed Emergency Financial Manager in Benton Harbor, which unbeknownst to Pinkney, was a no-no:

> I remember the first time, back in 2009, we marched against the Emergency Manager. I get a call from the state saying, "You can't march on him. That's a direct action!" And I'm listening to

this nut, and I'm thinking, I'm supporting a march on the Emergency Manager. You're not going to tell me who I can support and who I can't support! And we had just started; we had just got out there…

Rev. Pinkney was quickly finding out which way the political wind blew, although it would be some time before he knew who was generating it. The response of the organization already didn't sit well with him and things would only get weirder:

We were having a memorial for T-Shirt, the guy who was killed on the motorcycle back in 2003. The vice president of the state NAACP, I guess he must have had the national blessing to come down and spy on us. He was hiding in the bushes, spying on us for about two hours. He was laying on his belly and watching what we were doing. I believe it was someone from the ACLU that first spotted him. They said, "There's someone over there; they've been over there a long time watching you." I didn't pay it no attention; I figure everybody's watching…I don't care about that; they can spy all they want. It's not going to stop us from doing what we're doing.

First comes the spying, then comes the divorce. The reverend says he has "friends in Detroit" who told him that the Whirlpool Corporation approached the NAACP and expressed a desire to contribute, but not if Pinkney remained president of the Benton Harbor chapter. It was shortly thereafter, he says, that he received an email from the state level accusing him of not conducting regular meetings, and then another saying there had never been a valid election. He knew both accusations were false and provided proof. The higher-ups pushed for a new election, and he was forced to take the distasteful step of suing the NAACP. His controversial action would bring him support from an unexpected quarter: past presidents of chapters around the nation.

> What I did, more than anything else, I got a group of former presidents across the country together. Most of them contacted me and they were saying they agreed with me and wanted to be a part of what I was doing. They liked that I was willing to take a stand, so of our group, they wanted me to be the president.

Besides honoring Pinkney's leadership abilities, they would also give him some vital clues to help fill in the bigger picture at the NAACP.

> These presidents of these other chapters said they found out the same way that I did that they were all working together. They've got their own little—it's like a social club. You can't get in that social club; you might be a president over here, but you can't get in unless they invite you in. If they don't invite you in, then you don't get a chance to sit down with them and see how it actually works; how the ball turns, how they keep everybody else in line.

Is Pinkney suggesting that most of us are sheep? I personally don't know the answer to that because I'm not too familiar with farm animals, but if I were to hazard a guess, I would say, "Yeah." However, like the creators of the US Constitution, he favors a healthy, open selection system to start with, and measures to prevent the concentration of power in a few hands. "That's where the board comes in," he says. "That's why a person should be elected by the members and not by that board, because if you're elected by that board, they still control you."

He says the group of former presidents filled him in on some past history as well. Apparently, the bylaws of the NAACP came straight out of MIT in Boston. "The bylaws were written by a CIA agent," he says, "and the way it's designed, if you step over this line, then we come in and remove you." It appears that the government has hit on an ingenious way to infiltrate, by becoming part of the very bones of the organization.

Such systems of control don't seem to welcome an independent spirit like Pinkney's. His reign would end after three years, the last year requiring a court battle to block two mid-term elections. When the regular election did come, he'd be squeezed out by a concerted effort from Whirlpool, the company offering a free membership in the NAACP to anyone who was willing to vote against Rev. Pinkney.

He has now severed his relationship with the NAACP and questions its relevance. "They're out of touch with our community," he says. He has burned his membership card and invited others he is in contact with to do the same. As of this writing, over ten thousand former members have burned their cards in response to the reverend's call, and he continues to win more converts when he tells his story.

It's a story of betrayal, and it's one that more and more Americans can identify with these days. It seems like we're being let down on all sides, in a hundred different ways. Name an institution and it seems like there is a recent smudge or scandal attached, from the Catholic Church to the National Security Agency. Companies are reneging on their pensions, banks are forcing people out of their homes, government employees are being found in the most compromising positions, and national organizations are selling their name to the highest bidder. It seems as if all of these institutions have reached their zenith; they can go no further. Yet, their evolution has only highlighted their dysfunction, making it increasingly clear that business as usual, in virtually any area, is about as insane as you can get.

For a person of color, the list gets longer and stronger: racial profiling by banks, insurance companies and other financial institutions, not to mention the police; gross overrepresentation in prisons and the justice system in general; discrimination by landlords and employers; substandard housing and schools—the list could go on and on. For black people especially, the American Dream has probably seemed like a lot of hooey for a long time. Maybe forever. Their betrayal has been more pronounced, more complete, and more obvious than any other, and there are still pockets of people in this country who are cheering that on. I believe Rev. Pinkney lives across the river from one of those pockets. When the reverend had the audacity to stand up and protest, it provoked a reaction of such viciousness and magnitude from that quarter it became the incentive for writing this book.

He continues to press on despite the obstacles, or perhaps because of them, and serves as an inspiration to those around him who are seeking to effect change. In Benton Harbor, the takeover by an unelected Emergency Manager remains a continual concern, and organizations like the school board need watching. He continues to broadcast his radio show weekly, acting as a sounding board for the oppressed and forgotten, the throwaways and the victims. Most recently, he's been dealing a lot with what are called "targeted individuals" or "TI's." These people claim to be specifically targeted by the government, allegedly using weapons and methods that would blow your mind. These stories, if true, suggest a government that has become Machiavellian to the point of erasing all humanity and embracing insanity. One hour of the heart-wrenching, stomach-twisting accounts is enough to make you either want to kill somebody or crawl somewhere and hide. But Pinkney, in his inimitable way, allows the light to fall on these dark areas, like any other.

Perhaps his greatest strength is that he seems to know his mission and pursues it with a passion that is inspiring. That mission has required him to play many roles: speaker, organizer, prisoner, educator, religious man, funny man, and so many more. Through his trials, he has shone the light on some dark places in the justice system and done it with an open heart and a sense of humor. My life is much richer for having known this funny reverend, this loving fighter, this streetwise, shining soldier of truth.

Afterword

The main text for this book was finished in 2013. However, due to lack of a publisher, it sat on a shelf for over two years. In that period of time Rev. Pinkney's fight has grown ever more challenging and his situation increasingly dangerous. As of this writing in early 2016, the courageous activist has already served more than eighteen months of a sentence that could span ten years, all because five dates appear to have been changed on a petition he was involved with to recall then-mayor of Benton Harbor, James Hightower.

Anybody who has circulated a petition knows the penalties for filling in wrong information are clearly spelled out in the fine print at the bottom of the form. The worst that can happen is a misdemeanor charge with a small fine and/or a few months in jail. That's what they gave to Mark Demet of Racine, WI, who actually filled in some signatures to make his quota.

But Rev. Edward Pinkney, as you may have come to notice, is different. He represents the dismantling of an antiquated power structure that no longer serves the majority of people, if it ever did. And the man cannot, will not stop fighting. He's just made that way. Add to this his religious principles and he becomes a force to be reckoned with.

Antiquated or not, power structures do their best to preserve their own existence, and that's why Rev. Pinkney has been dealt with so severely.

They came for him on April 24, 2014, his wife's birthday. Coincidence? Probably not. To arrest the minister, who at the time was sixty five, the authorities thought it prudent to send a fully dressed SWAT team. Luckily, the reverend was taking his wife out to dinner, as many good husbands do, so he missed the twenty or so ninja police prowling his street like they were searching for a drug overlord. (Perhaps the cops should have wandered over to now former mayor Hightower's house, whom, it is said, once fell into that category. But let's not talk trash.)

The next day Rev. Pinkney, armed with his lawyer, visited the police station and was arrested. The judge posted a $30,000 bond of which the reverend paid ten per cent to be on his way.

They took him to trial on October 27, 2014, his own birthday. Again, it doesn't take a statistician to realize this was not a coincidence. Those familiar with court tactics will recognize this for the psychological warfare that it is.

The jury selection process was handled in a similar way. Rev. Pinkney called it an all-white jury but, to be fair, there was a young Latina in the box. Otherwise he's right: eight young white women, most of whom appeared intelligent, and three balding white men with glasses who looked like they could have been relatives. Not one person of the same race as the reverend. In fact, he says, no one from Benton Harbor or Benton Township sat on that jury.

There was one other white guy, sitting in the alternate chair, who wore a turtleneck and looked like he might be cool, so to speak. But as luck (or something) would have it, right when it was time to deliberate the cool guy had to get on a plane going out west somewhere. It seemed odd at the time that one could get out of their jury commitment so easily, once the trial had started.

It was just another item on a long list of oddities. After ten years of watching this stuff, I could tell you some things. I could tell you a lot of things, but I run the risk of boring you or you simply not believing me. I find most of it hard to believe myself.

I still can't believe how the prosecutor put on a racist hat and derided Rev. Pinkney for being a public black leader, how he pranced around the courtroom like a choir director exhorting the jury to convict without evidence, and how the judge backed him up if he happened to slip or didn't come on strong enough.

Then there was the earnest young forensics expert. Sure, he was smooth and polished and looked directly at the jury when he answered the prosecutor's questions. And, yes, he seemed quite knowledgeable about methods to detect changes in ink. Nonetheless, in the final analysis, he didn't add a scrap to the evidence pile. (I say "pile" facetiously because evidence wasn't required and, therefore, didn't enter the picture.)

So it was a real jaw-dropper, to say the least, when the virtually all-white jury voted the reverend guilty of forgery, a serious crime that usually involves one copying another's signature and making off with a lot of money. It's a mystery as to what blinded the jury to the fact they were sending a man to prison for a very long time over a few date changes that could have been made by anyone, including authorities. But, as I said, I've been following Rev. Pinkney's fight for ten years now, and nothing surprises me anymore.

One thing I do know: Something is seriously wrong in Berrien County, Michigan.

If only that were the extent of it. Unfortunately, it appears the Berrien County justice system is just a seeping pustule in a much larger system that is cancerous with corruption. The 3rd District Court of Appeals is well aware of a previous unwarranted imprisonment of Rev. Pinkney by Berrien County officials, yet they seem loathe to act on his current appeal, which was filed months ago. Perhaps it will take the ACLU stepping up again to embarrass the court into doing the right thing.

Things just seem to get worse as you go up; calls to Michigan's governor might as well be made to a deaf-mute. To many in the state, this is no surprise. After all, if reports can be believed, Gov. Snyder wasn't concerned if the whole city of Flint drank lead; why would he care about one very vocal preacher in prison? Especially if he's the loudmouth who has been giving the boys over at Whirlpool so much trouble.

At this point, I'll ask the reader to forgive the sarcasm creeping in. This is my way of dealing with the inevitable bitterness that arises from recalling these events. It comes from too much time spent on hard benches in cold courtrooms where normalcy is like a breath of fresh air in a shit house. It comes, too, from looking in the eyes of well-dressed guys who use lies like lullabies. They sing the jury to sleep with them during the day and use them to comfort themselves at night. Maybe someday they'll realize the grave injustice they've done to a man who has helped so many. Then again, maybe they won't.

If courthouses were ever bastions of justice, they are something far different now.

Truth be told, Rev. Pinkney's case is just the tip of the iceberg. Quacy Roberts, a witness at Pinkney's trial, later told me that Berrien County was retaliating for his testifying by claiming he never graduated from high school. Yet he showed me his actual diploma and even some transcripts from college.

He also mentioned he had won over $100,000 in a settlement because a Benton Harbor policeman named Andrew Collins had planted drugs on him. Apparently Collins, along with his senior officer Bernard Hall, made quite a habit of doing this; Roberts said at least eighty other people had won settlements from the city for the same reason. Can you imagine that? We're talking about eighty people whose lives were ruined with jail time and other horrible things because two monsters in cop suits wanted to improve their career stats. What's worse, Roberts says the two were encouraged by higher-ups to secure more convictions. Sadly, almost nobody seems surprised by that kind of thing anymore.

Much more information about this story can be found on the Benton Harbor BANCO website, bhbanco.org. Just enter "drug planting" into the search engine.

This site is also the best source for information about Rev. Pinkney. It includes up to date information on his current whereabouts and circumstances. If you wanted to write him you could find his address there, and there are numbers to call to protest his treatment. A word to the wise: The website has become a bit ponderous so be selective about what you read. There are plenty of rants but also plenty of gems if you look around. The site is best taken in small doses; many of the articles are eye-openers and some of them will make you sick.

At this time, Rev. Pinkney's situation in prison appears tenuous and unpredictable. In a speech in Benton Harbor recently, the reverend's wife Dorothy said that in prison he is "...constantly harassed, threatened and intimidated by racist guards, phone privileges taken away by the warden, accused of smuggling information to me, incoming and outgoing mail is tampered with and he has had several bogus tickets written on him..." What she doesn't mention is that the reverend's phone privileges were revoked for six months because a reporter who interviewed him was merely walking out with some notes on the conversation, and each of the tickets he was given could mean time in a solitary unit.

The quote from Dorothy Pinkney was taken from the back page of the Peoples' Tribune, an independent monthly coming out of Chicago. Found on the internet at peoplestribune.org, it is a good way to stay connected to some of the struggles that are going on. The publishers are so supportive of Rev. Pinkney's cause that every month now for over ten years they have devoted the entire back page of the paper to what's going on in Benton Harbor. In their February, 2016 issue, they included an additional article inside about how they were able to visit the reverend in prison over the new year. It must have been quite a coup since, at the time, he was still not able to use the phone.

I could elaborate more on Rev. Pinkney's mistreatment, but maybe this is a good time to let you go. I've given you some good resources for further research, and besides, you've got your life, your mission, your reason for being here. It's probably time you got back to it.

You have made it this far in the book which suggests you are a trooper and open to hard truths. Maybe you are already an activist and I've been preaching to the choir the whole time. If you have been active for a while you realize that the more you do, the more you get asked to do, so please get out there and make those phone calls. And thanks for all you do—you are the ones who give life to the movement.

If you are a newbie, not wanting to stick your neck out too far, or just looking for something closer to home, start looking for activists in your area. Often badmouthed by the politicos, they are people who are already challenging the current system and working to bring in a saner one. You might see them doing "silly" things like walking in circles, carrying signs and singing in repeated chants. Get out of your car and walk closer to the protest, if you are not too busy. If you resonate with the issue, join in. And if you don't understand what they are asking for, pull one of them aside and ask them to explain. This activity alone will show that you at least support their willingness to get out and make a change happen in a peaceful way.

And don't think your voice doesn't count. Every new person in a protest means the word is spreading. If you support those who already fighting, you add strength and validity to their actions.

These pioneers, these early risers, want and need our support. They are waiting for us to catch up, to add to the energy that will finally turn the tide. Architects of an emerging paradigm, they are models of a new kind of citizen, ready to bring in a better world if we will only let them.

To contact the author
or to find out more
about Rev. Pinkney
visit
soldieroftruth.com

62446024R00069

Made in the USA
Lexington, KY
08 April 2017